Janet Hayward has over 15 years' experience in the beauty industry and is the co-founder of the beauty and health website, beautydirectory.com.au, which is followed by beauty experts worldwide. Originally from the United Kingdom, Janet now lives in Sydney, Australia with her family.

Susie Prichard-Casey is a natural beauty and body guru who holds advanced diplomas in Remedial Massage, Reflexology and LaStone Therapy. Susie has worked for Neal's Yard amongst other top London spas. Susie currently lives in Berkshire, England where she is busy studying beekeeping and developing her own honey and organic product range.

Arielle Gamble is a talented illustrator and art director and currently based in New South Wales, Australia. Arielle loves to work with ink and watercolours, and much of her work explores themes around the natural world.

First published in Great Britain in 2016 by Modern Books
An imprint of Elwin Street Limited
3 Percy Street
London W1T 1DE
www.elwinstreet.com

Copyright © 2016 Elwin Street Productions

All rights reserved. No part of this book may be used or reproduced in any manner whatsoever without written permission from the publisher except in the case of brief quotations embodied in critical articles or reviews.

ISBN 978-1-906761-78-3
10 9 8 7 6 5 4 3 2 1

Printed in China

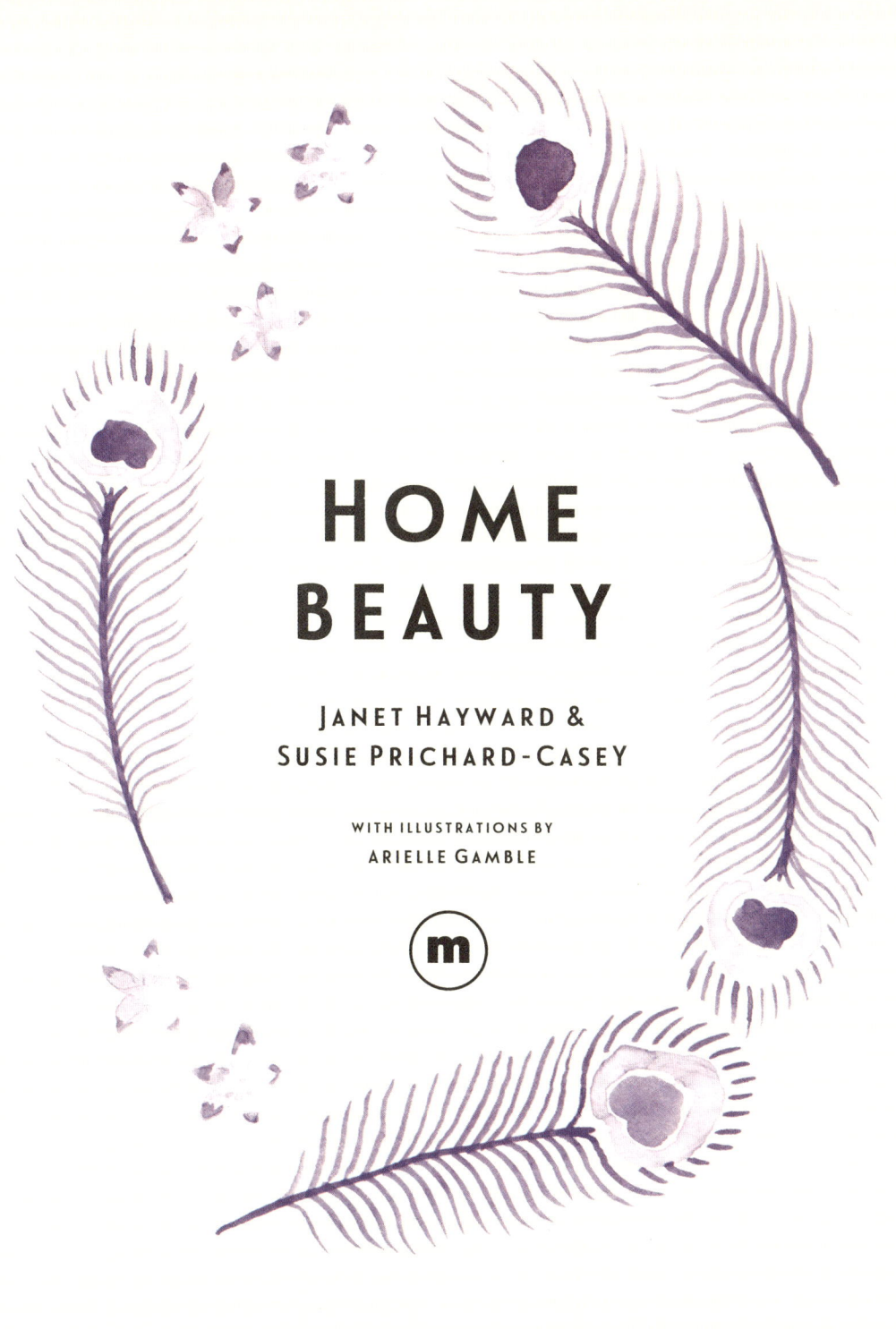

Home Beauty

Janet Hayward & Susie Prichard-Casey

with illustrations by Arielle Gamble

(m)

CONTENTS

Introduction	6
RADIANT SKIN	8
Green Tea Face Cleanser	10
Apple and Thyme Cleanser	10
Grapeseed and Borage Oil Cleanser	11
Gentle Rose Water Toner	12
Aloe Vera Moisturizer	13
Beeswax Moisturizer	14
Exfoliating Vibrancy Facial Scrub	16
Brightening Facial Peel	17
Natural Face Packs	18
Facial Mud Pack	19
Energizing Face Pack	20
Brightening Fruit Facial	22
Natural Eye Mask	23
Eye Bag Blitz	23
Strawberry Facial Steamer	24
Hydrating Coconut Oil Treatment	26
Natural Spot Treatments	27
BEAUTIFUL BODY	28
Sea Salt Skin Buffer	30
Making a Loofah	31
Almond and Oatmeal Scrub	32
Sugar Body Scrub	33
Home-Made Moisturizer	34
Intensive Dry Skin Balm	35
Lovely Legs Shaving Balm	36
Coconut and Lavender Body Cream	38
Cooling and Rejuvenating Face and Body Mist	39
Detoxifying Clay Body Mask	40
Body-Firming Tonic	41
Anti-Cellulite Body Tonic	42
Natural After-Sun Gel	44
Natural Deodorant	45
INDULGENT BATH TIMES	46
Rose Bath Milk	48
Bubble Bath	50
Sweet Almond Bubble Bath	51
Citrus Body Wash	52
Using Bath Salts	54
Chamomile Bath Salts	55
Bath Bombs	56
Bath Bags	58
Soothing Oatmeal Soak	59
Calming Lavender Bath Soak	60
Handmade Soap	61

HOLISTIC HAIR CARE	**62**
Home-Made Shampoo	64
Dry Shampoo	65
Home-Made Conditioner	66
Deep Conditioning Treatment	67
Protein Hair Pack	67
Glossing Treatment	68
Thickening Treatment	70
Mint Scalp Treatment	71
Vinegar Hair Rinse	71
Beer Hair Treatment	72
Chamomile Hair Rinse	73
Lightening Treatment	74
Darkening Treatment	76
Heat Protection	77
Root-Lift Booster	77
Beach Hair Salt Water Spritz	78
FINISHING TOUCHES	**80**
Lash Conditioner	82
Eyebrow Thickener	83
Teeth Whitener	84
Lip Buffer	85
Natural Lip Plump	85
Natural Powder Blush	86
Natural Lip Tint	87
Body Butter	88
Body Oil	88
Home Pedicure	89
Foot Exfoliator	90
Softening Foot Balm	91
Home Manicure	92
Nail Whitener	94
Cuticle Cream	94
Hand and Nail Cream	95
Nail Oil	96

SOOTHING SCENTS	**98**
Home-Made Perfume	100
Home-Made Cologne	101
Lavender Sachets	102
Aromatherapy	104
Home-Made Pillow Spritz	106
Aromatherapy Potpourri	107
Blending a Massage Oil	108
Basic Massage Blends	109
Index	*110*
Buyer's Guide	*112*
Safety Notes and Precautions	*112*

INTRODUCTION

Beauty is enjoying an artisanal revival with many beauty lovers turning to traditional, and often natural, ingredients to indulge in personalized hair treatments, beautiful body creams and bespoke facial products. Unlike mass-produced versions, these pamper products and treatments can work wonders on the mind, body and soul.

There is something indulgent and utterly pleasurable in making a treatment by hand that is especially for you. In this book you will find a wide range of DIY concoctions for the face, body, hands, feet and hair that you can make with everyday ingredients from your kitchen. With gorgeous recipes such as Beeswax Moisturizer (p. 14), Rose Bath Milk (p. 48) and Home Manicure (p. 92) we have you covered from top to toe. Treat yourself with a whole new, handcrafted beauty regime, create your own home spa for a girls' night in or spread the love with personalized, handmade pampering gifts for your family and friends.

Our skin is bombarded by the elements on a daily basis, which can take a real toll on its health and appearance. Natural ingredients and a little pampering will go a long way, and your skin will love you for it. This chapter has recipes for everyday use as well as indulgences for special occasions.

Green Tea Face Cleanser	Natural Face Packs
Apple and Thyme Cleanser	Facial Mud Pack
Grapeseed and Borage Oil Cleanser	Energizing Face Pack
	Brightening Fruit Facial
Gentle Rose Water Toner	Natural Eye Mask
Aloe Vera Moisturizer	Eye Bag Blitz
Beeswax Moisturizer	Strawberry Facial Steamer
Exfoliating Vibrancy Facial Scrub	Hydrating Coconut Oil Treatment
Brightening Facial Peel	Natural Spot Treatments

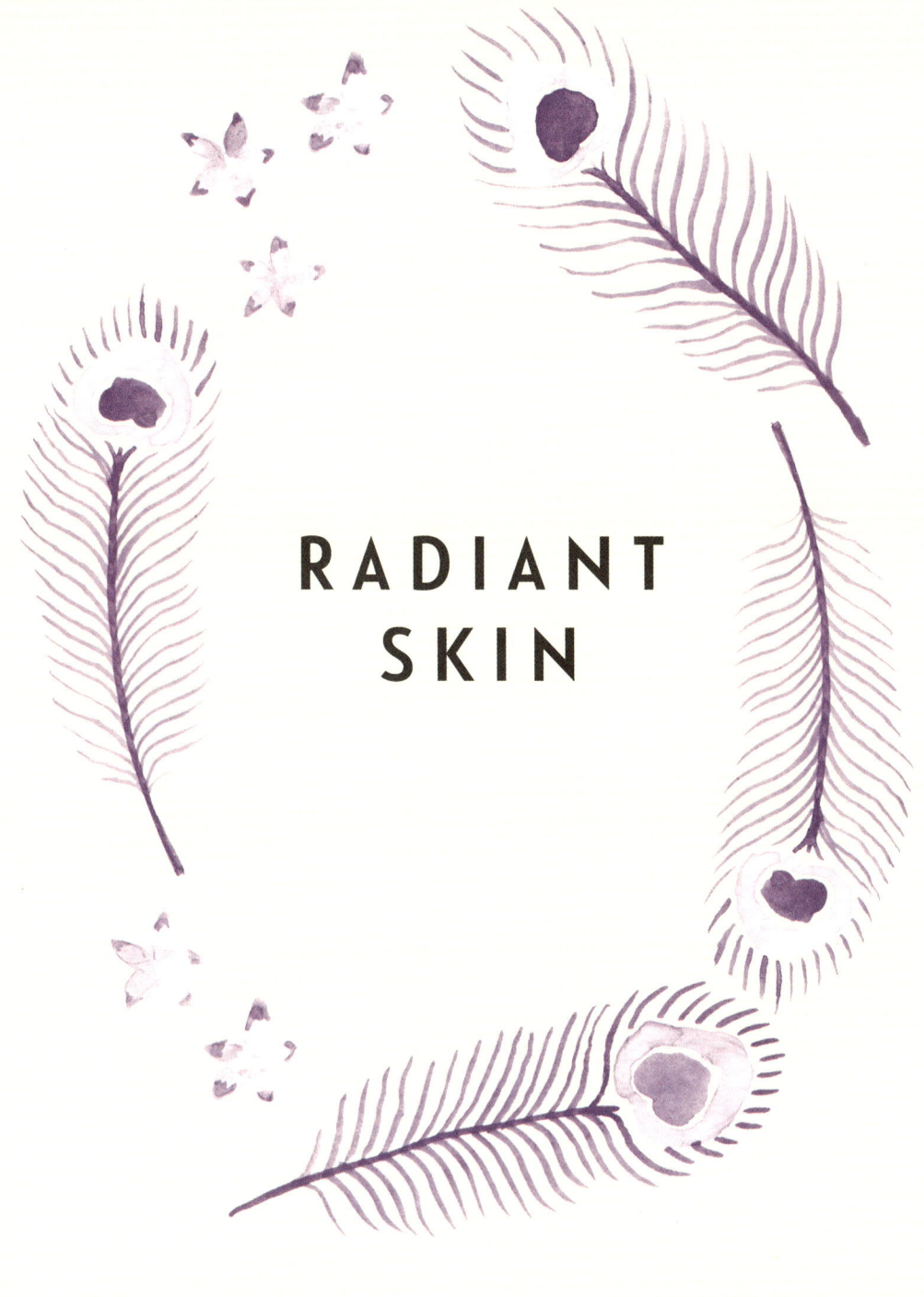

GREEN TEA FACE CLEANSER

Rich in polyphenols, which have a powerful antioxidant effect, green tea helps to reduce the free radicals that can cause premature ageing. Washing your face with this cleanser will remove dirt and dead cells while improving the texture and appearance of your skin. Prepare fresh each time.

2 teaspoons green tea leaves
spring water, freshly boiled
5 drops of jojoba oil
cotton wool pads

Place the green tea leaves in a small, clean cup and pour in 5 tablespoons of spring water. Leave to steep for 5 minutes.

Strain the tea into a small bowl and stir in the jojoba oil.

Dip a cotton wool pad into the green tea cleanser and sweep over your face, repeating with a clean cotton wool pad until the cleanser is used up. Use morning and night.

APPLE AND THYME CLEANSER

small bunch of fresh thyme
glass jar with lid
150 ml cider vinegar
3 teaspoons aloe vera gel
cotton wool pads

Finely chop the thyme and transfer to the glass jar. Pour the cider vinegar over the thyme, then close the jar lid tightly and place in the fridge.

Allow the mixture to infuse for one week, then strain and return to the glass jar. When ready to use, add one teaspoon of the base mixture to the aloe vera gel to make a cleanser. Apply with cotton wool pads, sweeping across face to cleanse.

GRAPESEED AND BORAGE OIL CLEANSER

Perfect for normal to dry and sensitive skins, this oil-based cleanser leaves skin feeling clean and velvety-smooth. Grapeseed oil is a light carrier oil with antioxidant properties, which is easily absorbed into the skin. Borage oil is rich in skin-loving gamma-linoleic acids that help soothe sensitive, inflamed or reactive skin.

*30 ml glass dropper bottle
grapeseed oil
borage oil
10 drops of essential oil, choose from:
   chamomile, to calm sensitive skin;
   lavender, to heal skin
     especially acne scars;
   rose, to improve texture and tone
     of dry or mature skin;
clean cotton face cloth*

Fill the glass bottle two-thirds full with grapeseed oil. Add enough borage oil to fill the bottle, and then add your chosen essential oil. Screw the top on the bottle and shake to blend.

To thoroughly clean your face and neck, use your fingers to massage in 3 drops of the cleanser, then use a damp cotton face cloth to gently wipe away the dust and grime of the day. Use morning and night.

For a deeper cleanse, rinse the face cloth in warm water and lay over the face for 3 minutes after massaging in the oil cleanser. Store in a cool, dark place, out of direct sunlight.

GENTLE ROSE WATER TONER

3 large handfuls of fresh rose
  petals, washed
ice cubes

You will need a large pan with a rounded lid, and the pan needs to be large enough for you to place a heatproof bowl inside it, and then put the pan lid on upside down. Ideally the bowl should not touch the bottom of the pan, so you will need something to act as a pedestal for the bowl to stand on, such as a smaller heatproof pan, dish or ramekin (or something heavy of a similar size).

Place the rose petals into the large pan around the pedestal, place the heatproof bowl on the pedestal and add just enough cold water to cover the petals.

Put the pan lid on upside down (if you only have a flat lid you can use a stainless steel bowl instead – it should be large enough to seal it but shallow enough so that its bottom does not touch the other bowl).

Turn up the heat to bring the water to a boil. Add the ice cubes into the inverted lid. As the rose-infused steam hits the underside of the cold lid, it will condense and drop into the internal bowl.

Turn the heat down and leave simmering gently for 2 to 4 hours. Every now and again, carefully lift the lid and take out a little distilled rose water, stopping when the rose scent of the liquid begins to weaken. Replace the ice and boiling water if needs be as you do this, and do not let the water boil dry.

ALOE VERA MOISTURIZER

Soothing, calming aloe vera makes an ideal moisturizer for normal to dry skin. For oily skin, use more aloe vera gel and less coconut oil. Coconut oil – a superfood – is easily absorbed into the skin and is rich in vitamin E. It helps to strengthen skin, improving elasticity and suppleness, and restoring a youthful glow. The addition of rose oil will increase the benefits of the moisturizer if your skin is dry, while a few drops of lavender have antiseptic and antibacterial properties for oily skin.

100 ml aloe vera gel
200 ml coconut oil
10 drops of rose or lavender essential oil
glass jar with lid

For normal to dry skin, blend the aloe vera gel with the coconut oil in a blender. Add your chosen essential oil and then blend again.

For normal to oily skin, blend two-thirds aloe vera gel with one-third coconut oil, plus three drops of your essential oil to form a more lotion-type consistency.

Pour into an airtight glass jar and store in the fridge. The moisturizer will solidify when chilled, so warm a small scoop of it in your palm before smoothing all over the body to moisturize and hydrate skin.

BEESWAX MOISTURIZER

This rich formula is ideal for the winter months, or if your skin is feeling tight and dry, as it is easily absorbed and leaves the skin nourished and comfortable. Beeswax (which can be bought online) provides a smooth consistency, while the olive oil, rich in antioxidants, helps to prevent premature skin ageing. Almond oil is rich in vitamins A, B and E, which nourish the skin, and the extra vitamin E helps to preserve the formulation. You can choose whether to add essential oils, such as ylang ylang (to smooth skin), geranium (to revitalize) or chamomile (to calm and soothe).

glass jar with lid
beeswax beads or pellets
olive oil
almond oil
4 vitamin E capsules
10 drops of essential oil (optional)

Fill the glass jar one-quarter full with the beeswax and fill the remaining three-quarters with equal quantities of olive oil and almond oil.

Stand the glass jar in a pan of hot water and stir until the mixture has melted. Remove the jar and allow to cool to room temperature, stirring occasionally.

Break open the vitamin E capsules and add the contents to the mixture, together with your chosen essential oil, stirring until all ingredients are combined.

The moisturizer is ready to use when cool. Store in a cool, dark place.

EXFOLIATING VIBRANCY FACIAL SCRUB

Perfect for normal to oily skin, this versatile cleansing scrub leaves skin free of dirt, grime and dead cells. The basil helps to lift greying cells and enlivens skin tone for the ultimate spring-clean effect, with fresh vibrant results.

pinch of salt
½ teaspoon cider vinegar
1 drop of basil essential oil
1 teaspoon ground almonds
1 teaspoon oat flakes (ground to a rough sand consistency with a pestle and mortar)

Thoroughly mix the salt, vinegar and basil essential oil together in a small bowl, then add the ground almonds and oat flakes.

Using your fingers, apply the mixture to the face in very gentle circular rolling patterns, focussing on the chin, nose and forehead, and taking care to avoid the eyes.

Rinse thoroughly, splashing with warm water, and gently pat dry before following with a moisturizer. Make fresh each time for best results and use the scrub twice weekly for consistently silky-soft, vibrant skin.

For a deep replenishment treatment, once a week, follow the scrub with a natural face pack and an intensive, rich moisturizer.

Try replacing basil with lemon essential oil to treat oily skin or comedones (blackheads) – it's a natural antibacterial and antiseptic purifier. Experiment using ground pulses in place of ground almonds.

BRIGHTENING FACIAL PEEL

Great for a deep cleanse and to enliven the complexion, this facial peel is rich in anti-ageing antioxidants thanks to the green tea, and will gently exfoliate and brighten with a vitamin C boost from the lemon. The honey helps to moisturize and tighten pores, assisted by the egg whites so that your skin is revived and brightened with an overall youthful glow. Make fresh each time.

1 teaspoon of green tea leaves
juice of ½ lemon
1 teaspoon honey
2 egg whites

Brew the green tea leaves in half a cup of water, and then add the lemon juice. Stir in the honey until it has dissolved. Set aside to cool, then strain and discard the tea leaves.

Add the egg whites to the cooled green tea mixture and stir thoroughly. Spread the peel evenly over the face, taking care to avoid the sensitive eye area – the lemon juice will give a tingling sensation as it works to exfoliate and brighten.

Leave for 30 minutes until the peel has dried and firmed, then gently roll off the face to remove old cells and ingrained debris. Rinse with warm water to reveal soft, smooth and evenly toned skin.

NATURAL FACE PACKS

Avocado Mask

Cut a ripe avocado in half, remove the stone and scoop the flesh out of the skins. Mash the flesh with a fork into a creamy pulp. Cover your face and leave for 15 to 20 minutes, then rinse off with warm water and spritz with toner to close the pores.

Strawberry Mask

Mash 4 to 6 strawberries with a fork and apply the pulp to your face (avoiding the eyes). Leave for 10 minutes, then rinse off with water or rose water, to leave your skin sparklingly beautiful.

Honey Scrub

Mix 1 tablespoon of honey with 2 tablespoons of finely ground almonds and ½ teaspoon of lemon juice. Rub gently over your face to exfoliate, then leave for 15 to 20 minutes before washing off.

FACIAL MUD PACK

This natural clay face pack will nourish and stimulate skin, lifting off dead cells, loosening comedones (blackheads), and clarifying skin tone and colour. Clay has absorbed the minerals of the earth for centuries and its natural ingredients provide a nourishing, soothing and calming weekly treatment. Rose oil is rich in nutrients that have an anti-inflammatory and hydrating effect on mature and problem skins. For dry or sensitive skin, apply a very fine layer of jojoba oil over your face before applying the mud pack. Make the pack fresh each time.

25 g green clay powder
1 teaspoon cornflour
1 teaspoon jojoba oil
1–2 teaspoons rose water
1 drop of rose essential oil

Combine the green clay powder and cornflour, and mix well. Mix the jojoba oil and rose water together, then mix in to the powder to form a smooth paste. Add the rose essential oil and thoroughly combine the ingredients.

Apply to the skin, avoiding the eye area, and leave for 15 minutes. Remove with warm water and gently pat dry.

Finish with a nourishing facial treatment oil, such as Hydrating Coconut Oil Treatment (p. 26) or an intensive moisturizer such as Beeswax Moisturizer (p. 14).

For oily skin, replace the rose essential oil with lavender and follow with an application of Aloe Vera Moisturizer (p. 13).

ENERGIZING FACE PACK

This fine clay-based mask is perfect for many skin types and helps to balance combination skin, soothes acne-prone skin, revitalizes dry skin and nourishes mature skin with its anti-ageing properties. Rich in calcium, magnesium, potassium and sodium, green clay energizes the skin and gently boosts lymph flow and circulation to increase oxygen to the skin. This face pack helps to soothe and heal the skin's surface, giving fresh, vibrant and perfectly smooth results. Your skin will improve in tone and colour after just one use. Make fresh each time and use once a week for best results.

25 g green clay powder
1 teaspoon cornflour
1 egg yolk
1 teaspoon brewer's yeast
1 teaspoon jojoba oil
1 drop of geranium essential oil

Combine the green clay and cornflour, and mix well. Add the egg yolk, brewer's yeast and jojoba oil, and add to the powder to form a smooth paste. Add the geranium oil and thoroughly re-mix.

Apply the mixture to the face and leave for 15 minutes. Remove with warm water and gently pat dry.

Finish with a nourishing facial treatment oil, such as Hydrating Coconut Oil Treatment (p. 26) or an intensive moisturizer like Beeswax Moisturizer (p. 14).

Try using a gentle facial scrub before applying the face pack, such as Exfoliating Vibrancy Facial Scrub (p. 16), then follow with a moisturizer.

BRIGHTENING FRUIT FACIAL

Fruit is rich in alpha hydroxy acids, which work as a natural exfoliator to melt away dead cells, helping to reinvigorate dull, aged skin, and improve texture and tone. Lactic acid in the milk powder has a similar effect, while also soothing and calming. Fruit is ideal for helping to improve the appearance of pigmentation, acne or pimple scarring, as well as helping fine lines and wrinkles. Perfect for all skin types, this facial can be tailored for the best results by selecting an astringent fruit for combination to oily skin or a soothing one for dry to sensitive skin. Make fresh each time.

6 tablespoons milk powder
1 tablespoon honey

for your preferred fruit, choose:
1 medium-sized banana, for dry to sensitive skin
6 strawberries, for combination to oily skin

Mash the banana or the strawberries in a small bowl and then add the milk powder and honey. Mix together until all the ingredients are thoroughly combined.

Smooth all over your face and neck using fingertips and leave for at least 10 minutes for the best results. Remove the mask with tissues before rinsing your face with warm water.

NATURAL EYE MASK

The skin around the eye area is fine and delicate, and can be easily irritated by the environment. When your eyes are feeling sore, red and tired an eye mask offers instant relief. This treatment is hydrating and soothing to help reduce puffiness and restore your natural sparkle. Make fresh each time.

1 teaspoon almond oil
2 tablespoons grated cucumber

Mix the almond oil with the grated cucumber in a small bowl. Apply one tablespoon of the mixture to each closed eye, lie back and relax. Leave for at least 5 minutes before washing off with cool water and gently patting dry.

EYE BAG BLITZ

Bags under the eyes can be a result of too much time in front of a screen, too much or too little sleep, or environmental stresses. No matter the cause, this recipe will help to blitz the puffy appearance of eye bags while hydrating the skin.

½ teaspoon coconut oil
2 cucumber slices

Massage the coconut oil around each eye in a gentle circular motion, starting at the top inner corner of the eye and sweeping around the eye socket to finish at the bottom corner.

Repeat the massage strokes several times, then place a cucumber slice over each eye and relax for 10 minutes. Repeat every evening if you can to keep eye bags at bay.

STRAWBERRY FACIAL STEAMER

A steam treatment is an ideal way to open and clean pores, and to hydrate the skin, making it more receptive to a facial oil or moisturizer. Strawberries have an invigorating effect, while chamomile is soothing and calming. This is a once-a-week treatment that is also great for de-stressing. Take special care to check that the steam is not too hot – it works even if you need to allow it to cool for a little longer.

4 strawberries
2 chamomile tea bags

Make two separate cups of chamomile tea and leave to infuse for 5 minutes. Mash the strawberries in a mixing bowl, then pour in the chamomile tea.

Boil the kettle and pour boiling water over the mixture to the half-full level of the bowl. Stand for 3 minutes, then cleanse skin as usual and tie back your hair.

Lean over the bowl – with your face at least 20 cm away from the water level – and cover your head completely with a towel to hold in the steam. Keep your eyes and mouth closed and breathe in the wonderful fragrance as the steam works on the skin.

After 5 minutes, remove the towel and splash your face with cool water to refresh and help close the pores. Finish with a favourite facial oil or moisturizer.

RADIANT SKIN

HYDRATING COCONUT OIL TREATMENT

This treatment is great for the colder months when skin appears dry and dull. Use it three times a week for dry to combination skin or once a week for oily or acne-prone skin. Coconut oil is not only a great hydrator and moisturizer, it also helps exfoliate dead cells to make skin smoother. It absorbs well to help reduce the appearance of lines and keep skin supple. This will keep for up to a week in the fridge.

3 tablespoons coconut oil
1 tablespoon cocoa or shea butter
10–12 drops lavender oil
glass jar with lid

Scoop the coconut oil into a glass bowl and add the cocoa or shea butter. Place the glass bowl into a pan of boiling water to melt. Combine the ingredients well, then remove the bowl from the heat.

Add the lavender oil and stir thoroughly as the mixture starts to cool. Pour into the glass jar and leave to cool before fitting the lid. Store in the fridge.

Use a teaspoon-sized amount of this treatment each time and warm in the palm of the hand before gently massaging all over your face and neck in circular movements, avoiding the delicate eye area. The treatment will absorb quickly, leaving your skin hydrated and glowing. Use all over the body too!

NATURAL SPOT TREATMENTS

BLACKHEADS

These are caused when the surface cells of blocked sebum glands come into contact with oxygen. Safely remove with a lavender essential oil facial steam to loosen the blackheads, followed by this treatment.

2 tablespoons spring water
1 teaspoon cider vinegar
2 drops of bergamot essential oil
2 drops of cypress essential oil
Cotton wool pads

Mix the spring water, cider vinegar and bergamot and cypress essential oils to produce a blackhead rinse.

Soak a cotton wool pad in hot water, add a drop of cider vinegar to the pad and sweep across the affected skin.

Gently squeeze the loosened blackhead, using tissues to avoid infection, then sweep across the area with a fresh cotton wool pad soaked in the comedone rinse.

PIMPLES

When a pore is completely congested a pimple will form. Apply the following treatment to the pimple to help reduce swelling and redness, and to help the skin heal.

2 evening primrose oil capsules
1 drop of camphor essential oil
1 drop of lemon essential oil
1 drop of lavender essential oil

Break open the capsules of evening primrose oil into a small dish and add the essential oils. Use your finger to gently dab a small amount of the mixture to the affected skin.

A drop of neat lavender oil can also be directly applied onto an emerging spot as a highly effective emergency treatment or to disinfect and heal unsightly bumps.

Nourish your body from top to toe with these natural scrubs, moisturizers and balms. The skin on your body, particularly your back often gets forgotten about and will benefit greatly from exfoliation and gentle moisturizing. These natural recipes will give you luscious soft skin.

Sea Salt Skin Buffer

Making a Loofah

Almond and Oatmeal Scrub

Sugar Body Scrub

Home-Made Moisturizer

Intensive Dry Skin Balm

Lovely Legs Shaving Balm

Coconut and Lavender Body Cream

Cooling and Rejuvenating Face and Body Mist

Detoxifying Clay Body Mask

Body-Firming Tonic

Anti-Cellulite Body Tonic

Natural After-Sun Gel

Natural Deodorant

SEA SALT SKIN BUFFER

To avoid blemishes and spots on your back, small bumps on your arms or dry patches anywhere on the body, it's important to exfoliate. The combination of sea salt and coconut oil gently scrubs away dead cells and polishes your skin to leave it smooth and hydrated. Add a favourite essential oil and it becomes a relaxing and enjoyable treatment once a week. Store in the fridge.

4 tablespoons coconut oil
2 tablespoons sea salt flakes
5 drops of essential oil, choose from:
 peppermint, to invigorate and refresh;
 citrus, to brighten;
 lavender, to soothe and calm;
glass jar with lid

For a single treatment, combine the coconut oil and sea salt, and mix thoroughly in a bowl. Add your essential oil to gently fragrance, then use straight away.

For a larger quantity, double or triple the amount of ingredients, and when mixed, spoon into the glass jar and store in the fridge.

Massage the skin buffer all over the body in upward, sweeping movements always towards the heart. Take care to massage more gently across the delicate décolleté and neck areas.

Rinse in a warm shower and gently pat dry. Your skin will feel smooth and soft without the need of a moisturizer.

BEAUTIFUL BODY

MAKING A LOOFAH

A loofah is actually the dried centre of a plant called the sponge or luffa – which looks like a long, slim pumpkin. This loofah, however, is made from fine muslin fabric, which is gentler on the skin and can be washed in the regular laundry to keep it fresh.

a piece of natural muslin measuring about 30 x 150 cm
cotton thread
needle
rubber band
thin cord, for hanging

This loofah can be hand-sewn or machine-stitched. Start by folding the fabric in half lengthways. Sew along the length and along one of the ends to leave an opening at the top.

Turn inside out and sew along the last open edge, leaving a long rectangle. Starting from the short edge, gather the material together, bunching it in one hand, then pinch it in the middle of the bunch.

Fix this bunched position with a rubber band, leaving 'puffs' of fabric on either side. Wrap the cord around the middle just above the rubber band and tie very tightly, leaving enough cord length to hang the loofah in the shower.

Snip off the rubber band and the loofah is ready to use to massage, cleanse and smooth your skin in the shower or bath.

ALMOND AND OATMEAL SCRUB

Skin – especially on your back – can become prone to blemishes and look dull if dead cells are allowed to build up. Here are two body scrubs that will slough away any debris to restore tone and vitality, while boosting circulation and ensuring fresh, smooth skin that is free of spots.

1 tablespoon ground almonds
1 tablespoon oatmeal
2 drops of lavender essential oil
1 vitamin E capsule

Combine the ground almonds, oatmeal and lavender oil in a bowl, then break open and add the vitamin E capsule, mixing thoroughly.

Apply the paste to the body in sweeping circles, paying particular attention to the back and also the heels, ankles, knees and elbows. Rinse off in the shower, pat dry and apply a natural body oil.

For very oily or blemished skin, replace the vitamin E and lavender oil with ½ teaspoon of jojoba oil and 1 drop each of lemon and rosemary essential oils.

For dry skin, replace the vitamin E and lavender oil with ½ teaspoon of evening primrose oil and 2 drops of rose essential oil.

SUGAR BODY SCRUB

Bring the luxury of a spa treatment into your everyday life with this deliciously indulgent body scrub that cleanses and soothes the skin.

250 g brown sugar
250 g avocado oil
2 teaspoons aloe vera gel
2 drops of lavender essential oil

Combine all the ingredients in a bowl. Scoop some of the scrub out using your hand and massage gently onto your skin for a minute (the scrub will tighten onto your skin like a mask). Leave on for 3 to 4 minutes before rinsing. The scrub can be used all over your body and is suitable for most skin types.

If you don't have the above ingredients, you can just add sugar to any cleanser for a moisturizing exfoliating scrub for smooth skin.

HOME-MADE MOISTURIZER

Wheatgerm oil contains natural preservatives as well as antioxidants, which brings an obvious extra boost to any home-made moisturizer. Avocado is an ideal treatment for tired or dry skin as it contains many of the oils lost through everyday life.

4 teaspoons wheatgerm oil
4 tablespoons avocado oil
280 g cocoa butter
1 teaspoon beeswax
½ teaspoon borax powder
2 tablespoons rose water
10 drops of geranium essential oil
5 drops of frankincense essential oil
5 drops of sandalwood essential oil

Combine the wheatgerm and avocado oils in a heat-resistant bowl and place in a pan that has been half-filled with water.

Place the pan over a medium heat, add the cocoa butter and beeswax to the bowl, and warm until the mixture has blended.

Dissolve the borax in the rose water and add to the mixture by stirring all the ingredients together. Remove the pan from the heat and add the essential oils.

Allow to cool before storing.

INTENSIVE DRY SKIN BALM

During the cold, windy winter months, even normal skin can become dehydrated and develop sore, dry, flaky patches. This intensive skin treatment is rich and nourishing for the driest skin, helping to replenish moisture and ensure skin is restored to optimum health. Use on the face and the body. Store in a glass jar in the fridge.

15 ml beeswax pellets
30 ml sweet almond oil
30 ml coconut oil
1 teaspoon rosehip oil
1 vitamin E capsule
8 drops of lavender oil
glass jar with lid

Place the beeswax pellets, almond oil, coconut oil and rosehip oil into a heatproof bowl, break open and add the vitamin E capsule.

Melt the ingredients together in the bowl over a pan of hot water, then add the lavender oil. Remove from heat and pour the mixture into a blender or use a hand blender to thoroughly mix. Keep blending the mixture as it cools until it thickens to a light and creamy texture.

When completely cool, spoon into the glass jar. Massage a small amount over dry patches as an emergency treatment or use as a regular face or body moisturizer.

LOVELY LEGS SHAVING BALM

This shaving balm is not just for lovely legs – it's a unisex formulation that can ensure a smooth, close shave for men too. The nutrient-rich ingredients will moisturize skin, while the Castile soap (a fine soap made with olive oil and soda) allows the shaving blade to glide easily over legs, underarms, face and even the bikini line, to avoid rashes or nicks in the skin. Store in a glass jar in the fridge.

3 tablespoons coconut oil
3 tablespoons shea butter
2 tablespoons jojoba oil
2 tablespoons liquid Castile soap
glass jar with lid

Melt the coconut oil and shea butter in a glass bowl over a pan of hot water. Add the jojoba oil and mix thoroughly before removing from the heat.

Leave to cool and then place in the fridge to set. Once solid, leave to soften slightly and break up with a spoon, then blend with a hand blender until the mixture becomes light and fluffy.

Add the liquid Castile soap and blend to combine. Spoon the mixture into the glass jar and store in the fridge.

This formulation is beautifully rich, and only a little is required to spread over the area before shaving, resulting in silky-smooth skin.

BEAUTIFUL BODY

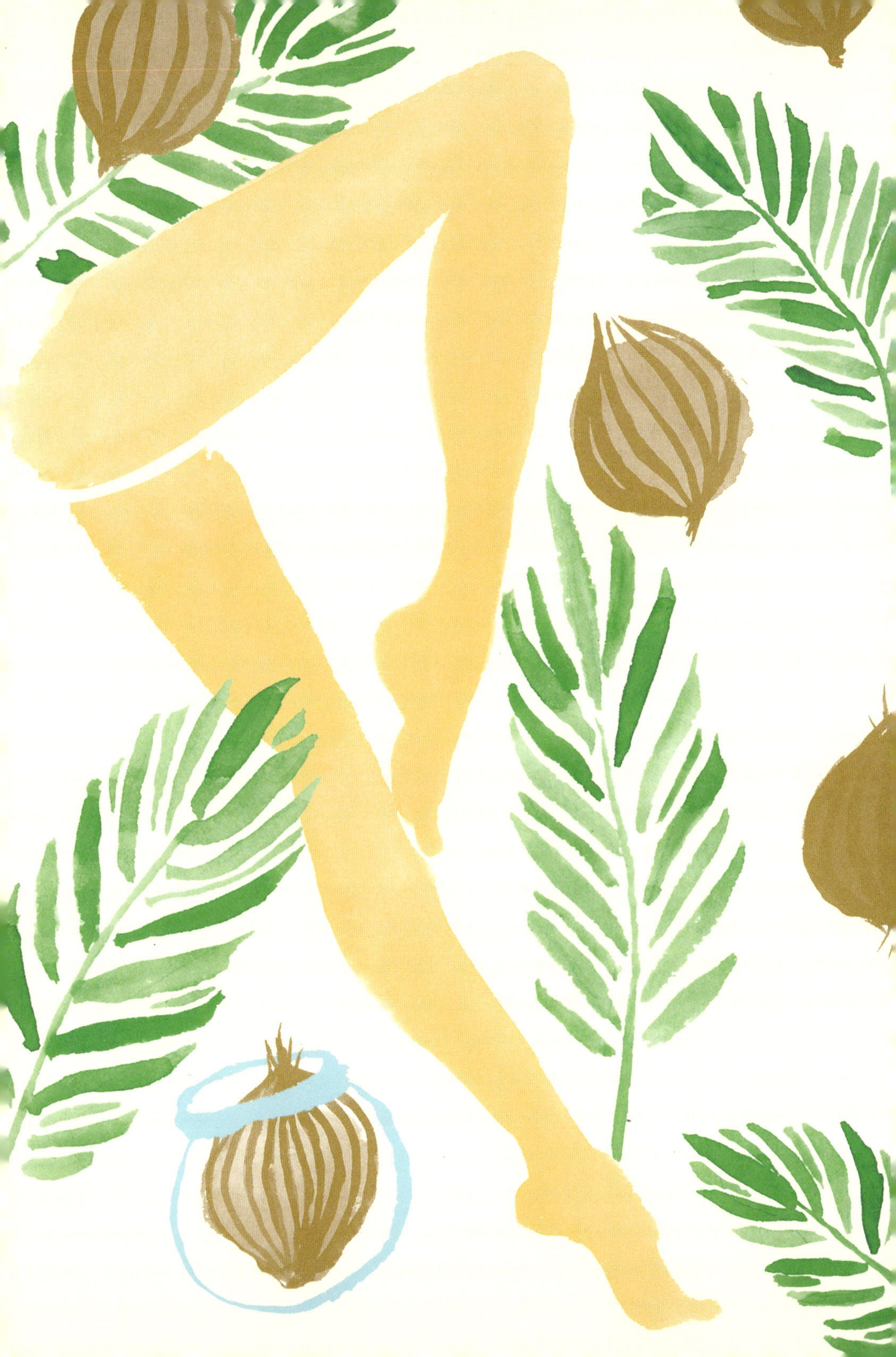

COCONUT AND LAVENDER BODY CREAM

Nourish all skin, even sensitive types, with this super-hydrating ointment. Lavender oil revitalizes the skin and its antiseptic properties helps to clear up acne and other blemishes.

250 ml coconut oil
4 drops of lavender oil
glass jar with lid

Spoon the coconut oil into a glass bowl and place over a saucepan of boiling water to melt the oil. Add the lavender oil and combine thoroughly, then remove from the heat.

Allow to cool and firm up, until almost solid. Then, using a hand blender or manual whisk, beat the mixture until it becomes light and creamy. Spoon into the jar and seal, ready to use.

COOLING AND REJUVENATING FACE AND BODY MIST

Soothe and enliven both face and body with this refreshing, mineral-rich mist. Cucumber cleanses and hydrates, improving the complexion of your skin and restoring your natural glow.

2 cucumbers
cotton muslin cloth
80 ml rose water
100-ml capacity spray bottle

Wash the cucumbers and finely grate them into a glass bowl. Strain the mixture through the muslin cloth into a second glass bowl to extract the cucumber water. Combine with the rose water, then pour into the spray bottle.

Spray over the face and body to condition and cool throughout the hot summer months.

DETOXIFYING CLAY BODY MASK

Like a facial mud pack, a body wrap will remove impurities and improve the texture and tone of your skin. Popular in spa resorts, a body wrap can form part of a beneficial luxury home spa ritual combined with a facial and aromatherapy bath. The green clay base is highly absorbent and draws toxins out of the skin, activating lymph and blood circulation to tone and reduce cellulite.

200 g green clay powder
1 egg yolk
5 drops of lemon essential oil
5 drops of rosemary essential oil
thin plastic sheeting (optional)

This treatment can be messy, so apply before stepping into the bath or shower. For a more relaxing treatment, cover a bed with plastic sheeting and recline as the body mask pampers your body.

Gradually mix the green clay powder with enough cold water to make a smooth paste. Add the egg yolk and the lemon and rosemary oils. Mix together with the green clay and apply smoothly all over the body.

Relax for 15 minutes, then sponge off with tepid water and thoroughly rinse in the shower. Your skin is now receptive to the nourishing benefits of an aromatherapy body oil.

BODY-FIRMING TONIC

The essential oil blend in this tonic will leave your skin feeling soft, clean and toned with a fresh-scented fragrance, and is perfect for use post-shower as part of a diet or detox regime to stimulate the lymphatic system and the senses. Take care with sensitive or dry skin as the alcohol may cause slight irritation. Store in a dark-glass pump spray bottle, away from direct sunlight.

dark-glass pump spray bottle
18 drops of lemongrass essential oil
2 drops of basil essential oil
4 drops of black pepper essential oil
5 drops of patchouli essential oil
10 ml high-proof vodka
100 ml cider vinegar
500 ml spring water
paper coffee filter

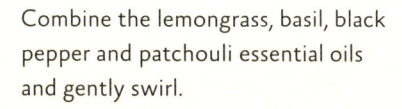

Combine the lemongrass, basil, black pepper and patchouli essential oils and gently swirl.

Add the vodka, shake well, then add the cider vinegar. Allow to settle for 24 hours, then add the spring water and shake well.

Strain through a paper coffee filter and pour back into the bottle. Spritz and massage into the skin on your thighs, buttocks and backs of arms to firm and tone for smooth, silky results.

ANTI-CELLULITE BODY TONIC

This body tonic is an effective formulation to combat poor circulation, sluggish areas of toxin deposits and fatty tissue. It works best if your skin is prepared first with a full body brush or clay body wrap to receive the full benefits of the invigorating and skin-conditioning ingredients. Perfect after a shower or as part of a diet or detox regime. Avoid use on sensitive or dry skin as the alcohol may cause slight irritation. Store in a dark-glass spray bottle away from direct sunlight.

10 drops of basil essential oil
6 drops of thyme essential oil
14 drops of grapefruit essential oil
10 ml high-proof vodka
100 ml cider vinegar
500 ml spring water
paper coffee filter
large dark-glass spray bottle

Add the basil, thyme and grapefruit essential oils into the spray bottle and swirl together.

Pour in the vodka, shake, then add the cider vinegar. Allow to settle for 24 hours, then add spring water and shake well.

Pour the contents through a paper coffee filter and then back into the dark-glass spray bottle. Spritz thighs, hips, buttocks and backs of arms to purify and tone cellulite areas.

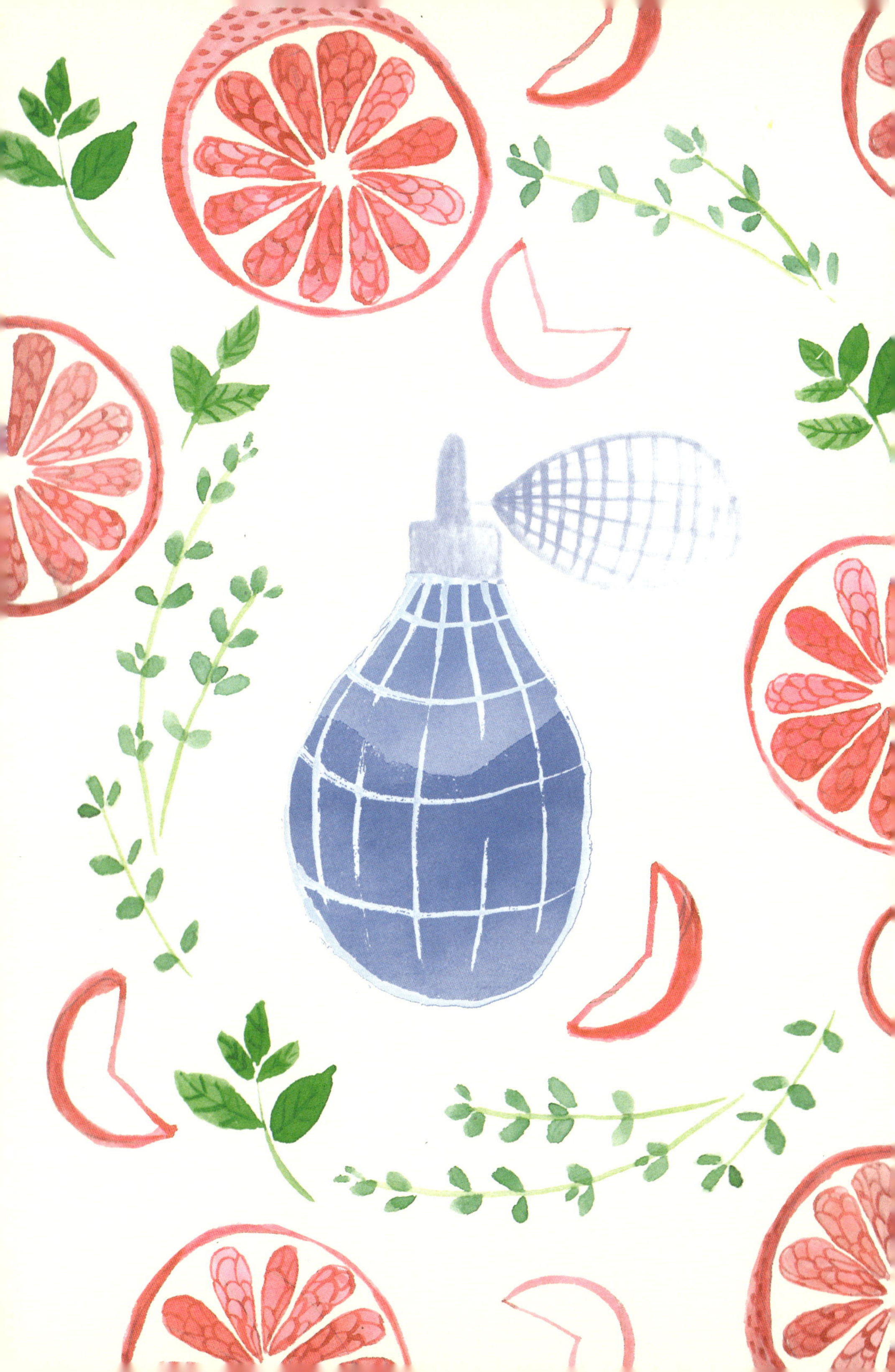

NATURAL AFTER-SUN GEL

After a day in the sunshine, skin can feel parched and roughened, especially after a trip to the beach. Use this soothing, anti-inflammatory and super-hydrating treatment to help replenish your skin. Make fresh each time.

30 ml aloe vera gel
10 ml jojoba oil
10 ml sweet almond oil
10 drops of chamomile essential oil
10 drops of geranium essential oil
10 drops of lavender essential oil
2–3 evening primrose oil capsules

In a small glass bowl mix together the aloe vera gel with the jojoba oil, sweet almond oil and the essential oils.

Break open the evening primrose oil capsules and add to the bowl. Mix again to combine.

After a cool shower to rinse away any sunscreen, gently pat the skin dry and then liberally apply the after-sun mixture all over the body, allowing full absorption before wearing clothes.

For slightly sunburned areas of skin, try cooling the area with ice cubes for at least 10 minutes to reduce the heat, then apply a drop of undiluted lavender oil directly to the skin. Always seek medical help for severe sunburn.

NATURAL DEODORANT

This spritz deodorant tonic is an easy-to-make, invigorating splash that works as a natural bactericide thanks to the combination of essential oils. A healthy and effective alternative to conventional deodorants, this formulation keeps the body feeling fresh with a delicious, clean aroma. Store in a large dark-glass pump spray bottle away from direct sunlight.

Large dark-glass pump spray bottle
10 drops of lavender essential oil
5 drops of lemon essential oil
5 drops of rosemary essential oil
5 drops of sage essential oil
5 drops of peppermint essential oil
10 ml vodka
100 ml cider vinegar
500 ml spring water
paper coffee filter

In the pump spray bottle, add all the essential oils, gently swirl, then add the vodka and shake well.

Next, add the cider vinegar and allow to settle for 24 hours. Add the spring water and shake well before filtering through a paper coffee filter and pouring back into the spray bottle.

Spritz under your arms after showering to keep fresh and deodorized – although take care if using after hair removal as the mixture may sting or cause irritation.

A long, hot bath is one of life's rare pleasures, so make it a truly luxurious affair with these delicious bath time treats. Tantalize the senses with essential oil bubble bath and float into a world of your own with soothing soaks and salts. Natural recipes to enliven your everyday shower experience are also included.

Rose Bath Milk	Bath Bombs
Bubble Bath	Bath Bags
Sweet Almond Bubble Bath	Soothing Oatmeal Soak
Citrus Body Wash	Calming Lavender Bath Soak
Using Bath Salts	Handmade Soap
Chamomile Bath Salts	

INDULGENT BATH TIMES

ROSE BATH MILK

Luxuriating in a deep, warm bath is one of the most relaxing and therapeutic experiences there is. This milk bath is a sensory delight that brings the spa into the home, leaving your skin feeling soft and moisturized, and your mind and body relaxed thanks to the Epsom salts and essential oils. Store in an airtight container away from direct sunlight. Epsom salts are available from chemists and pharmacies.

200 g powdered milk
120 g Epsom salts
12 drops of Rose Maroc essential oil
20 g dried rose petals
glass jar with lid

Combine the milk powder with the Epsom salts in a glass bowl, then add the rose essential oil and dried rose petals. Mix together thoroughly, then seal in an airtight container.

Run a deep, warm bath and drop in a handful of the bath mixture. As the air fills with the scent of roses, step into the luxurious, silky bath for the ultimate in relaxation.

INDULGENT BATH TIMES

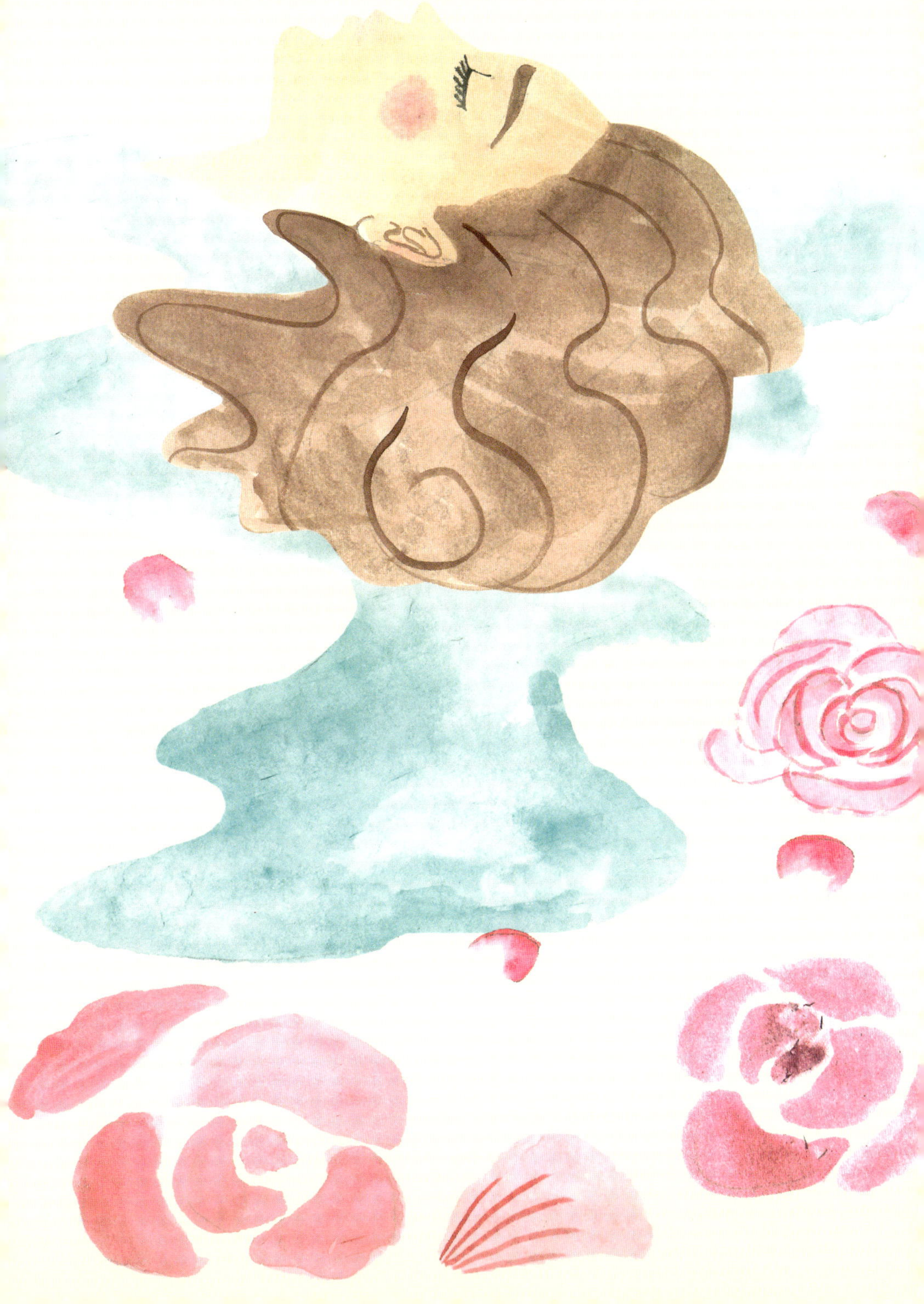

BUBBLE BATH

Remember how much fun a bubble bath can be? Try this home-made treat and bring a giggle back to your bath time.

150 g Castile soap, grated
200 ml distilled or filtered water
10 ml glycerine
5 drops of your chosen essential oil(s)
dark-glass bottle with cap

Dissolve the grated soap in the water; gently heating it first will speed the process. Alternatively, your can use liquid Castile soap.

Mix in the glycerine. Ingredient quantities can be varied depending on the desired amount and consistency.

Add your chosen essential oil(s). Lavender or rose are good for relaxation; peppermint or eucalyptus for stimulation.

Store in a dark-glass bottle for at least 24 hours. To use, shake gently and pour a generous amount under hot running bath water.

SWEET ALMOND BUBBLE BATH

This bubble bath will gently cleanse and moisturize skin with the added benefits of aromatherapy to calm the mind – particularly effective during times of stress or to generate a sense of well-being in the chillier months. The order essentials oils are added to a blend can change the properties and overall fragrance of the blend.

1 tablespoon witch hazel
200 ml sweet almond oil
dark-glass bottle with cap
100 ml liquid Castile soap
20 drops of frankincense essential oil
70 drops of lavender essential oil
30 drops of geranium essential oil
25 drops of ylang ylang essential oil
15 drops of patchouli essential oil
20 drops of chamomile essential oil

Mix the witch hazel and sweet almond oil in the bottle and shake vigorously to mix.

Slowly pour in the liquid Castile soap then add the essential oils in the following order to achieve a balanced fragrance: frankincense, lavender, geranium, ylang ylang, patchouli and chamomile.

Shake to mix well. For each bath, pour just 2 teaspoons under warm running water to release the aromas of the oils in foaming bubbles. Store the bottle out of direct sunlight.

CITRUS BODY WASH

This zesty lemon body wash is a great way to wake up the senses during a morning shower! The fresh and tangy fragrance enlivens your mind, while your skin benefits from the nourishing benefits of the oils and the antibacterial properties of the honey. All citrus fruit essential oils work well in this preparation, so use orange or grapefruit if you prefer. Store in a glass bottle out of direct sunlight.

4 tablespoons liquid Castile soap
glass jar with lid
1 tablespoon honey
1 tablespoon jojoba oil
20 drops of lemon essential oil
5 drops of spearmint essential oil
4 vitamin E capsules

Pour the liquid Castile soap into the glass jar and add the honey, jojoba oil, lemon essential oil and spearmint essential oil. Swirl to mix, then break open and add the vitamin E capsules.

Screw on the lid and shake well to combine the ingredients. Pour a little body wash onto a loofah or into the palm of your hand and enjoy the energizing scented lather as it cleanses and moisturizes.

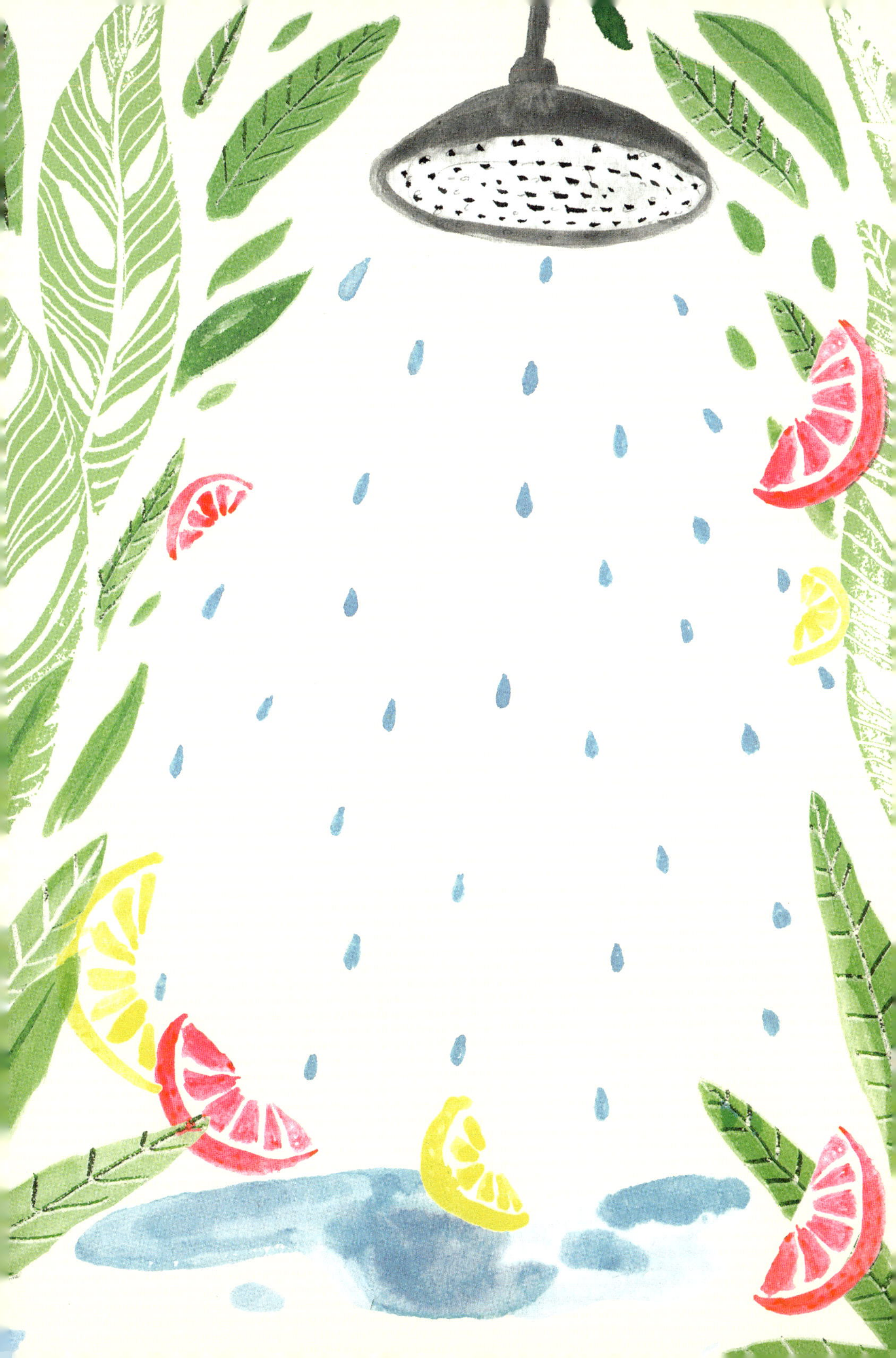

USING BATH SALTS

When you are physically tired and your muscles are aching, there's nothing quite like a long soak in a hot bath. The addition of home-made bath salts can make the experience all the more luxurious and beneficial.

ESSENTIAL OILS

rose: for moisturizing and even skin tone

lavender: to soothe with antiseptic and antibacterial benefits

ylang ylang: to promote smooth skin

geranium: to revitalize skin

thyme: to tone and refresh

evening primrose: to nourish and moisturise

lemon and citrus: to brighten

peppermint: to invigorate and refresh

chamomile: to calm sensitive skin

bergamot: to soothe and relax

sandlewood: to soften and restore

Simply add a drop or two of your favourite essential oil(s) and a handful or two of Epsom salts to your running bath water. The salts help to relax the muscles and eliminate toxins from the body, while the oils add a touch of heavenly aromatherapy.

If you want to upgrade from standard Epsom salts, deluxe options includes: sparkling, high-quality Ultra Epsom Salt and Himalayan salt – a lovely pale pink salt said to contain some 84 minerals needed by the body!

CHAMOMILE BATH SALTS

Soothe sensitive skin with this relaxing bath time treat. For an ultra soothing, mind-calming and relaxing bath that will also help improve circulation and tone skin, add the rosemary sprigs at the same time as the chamomile tea bags and allow to infuse before stepping into the bath.

250 g Epsom salts
4 chamomile teabags or 2 tablespoons chamomile flowers tied in a muslin cloth
2 sprigs of fresh or dried rosemary (optional)

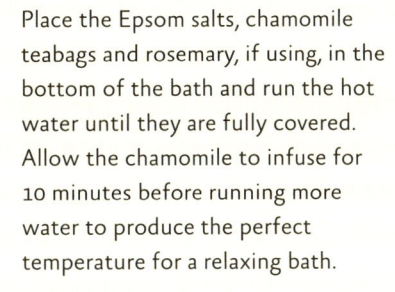

Place the Epsom salts, chamomile teabags and rosemary, if using, in the bottom of the bath and run the hot water until they are fully covered. Allow the chamomile to infuse for 10 minutes before running more water to produce the perfect temperature for a relaxing bath.

For the maximum benefit, leave the teabags or muslin cloth in the bath as you relax before bedtime and enjoy a restful beauty sleep.

BATH BOMBS

The fizzing aroma of bath bombs makes bedtime fun for children and adults alike, and the bombs are really easy to make. The pretty pastel colours bombs, studded with petals and herbs, make lovely bathroom ornaments too. Bath bombs can be moulded into different shapes, or use a silicon ice-cube tray to make miniature bath treats. Store in an airtight container.

10 ml spring water
spray bottle
50 g citric acid
100 g bicarbonate of soda
8 drops of essential oil, choose from:
  lavender
  rose
  ylang ylang
2 drops of natural food colouring
5 g petals or herbs, choose:
  rose petals
  rosemary
  lavender
silicon ice-cube tray or moulds
rubber gloves

Pour the spring water into the spray bottle.

Mix the citric acid and bicarbonate soda in a plastic bowl. Make a well in the centre and add the essential oil and colouring, together with the dried petals or herbs. Mix all the ingredients together thoroughly to disperse any lumps.

Spritz water from the spray bottle into the bowl 10 times. Working quickly, press the mixture into the ice-cube tray or moulds, or work into the desired shapes before it hardens.

Leave overnight to thoroughly set. When dry, pop out of the tray or moulds and store in an airtight container. Drop a bath bomb into a warm bath and enjoy the fizzing aroma and pretty scattering of petals or herbs in the bath!

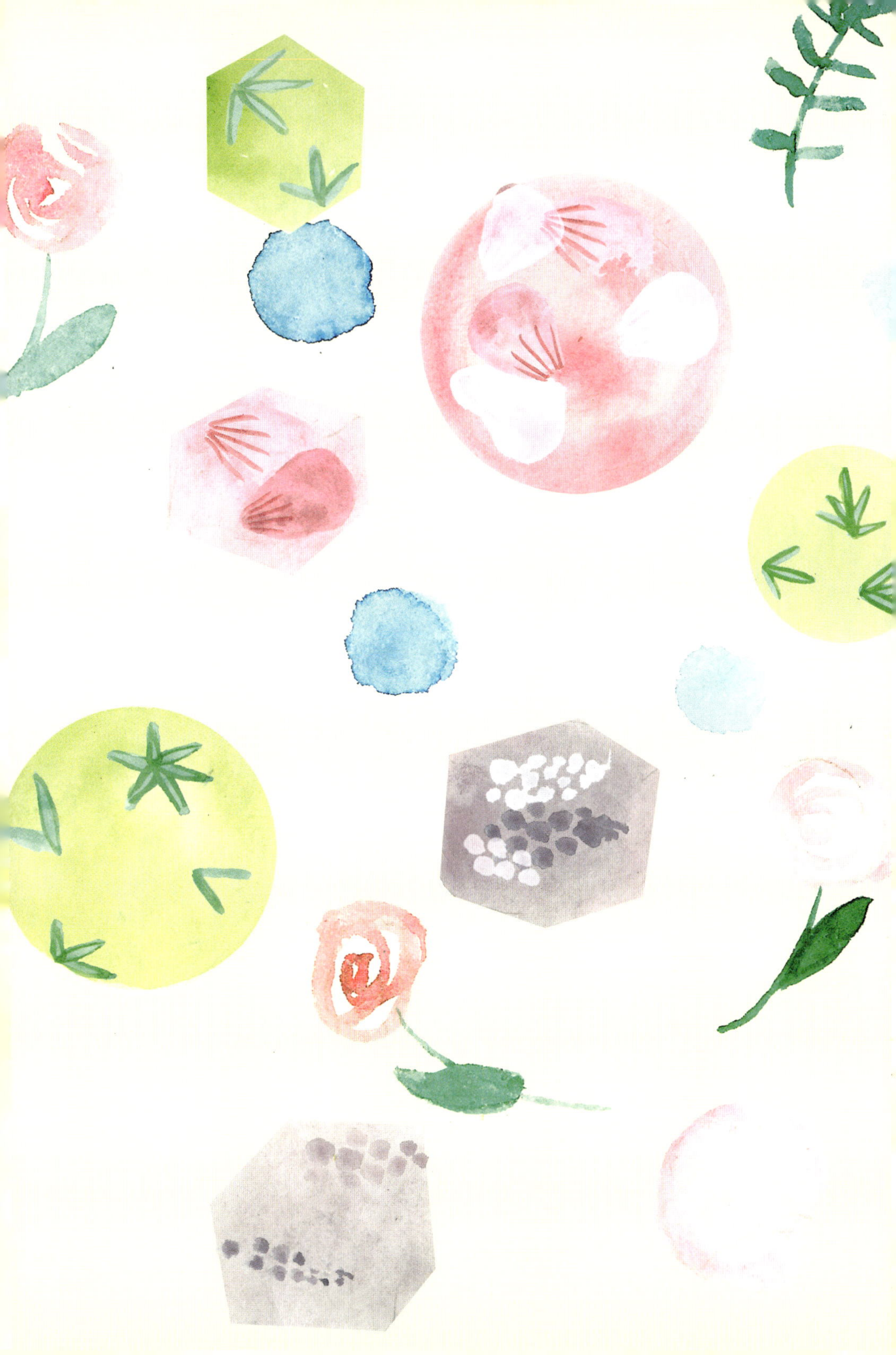

BATH BAGS

Recreate a luxury spa experience at home with these bath bags, adding skin-enhancing, therapeutic benefits to a deliciously scented bath. The bag can be left in the bath or removed after 5 minutes, depending on personal preference.

2 x 15-cm squares of natural muslin (or a ready-made spice bag)
cotton thread
needle
2 tablespoons coconut oil
3 tablespoons milk powder

for an invigorating bath
1 teaspoon dried basil leaves
3 drops of lemongrass essential oil

for a nourishing and hydrating bath
1 teaspoon dried rose petals
3 drops of rose essential oil
3 vitamin E capsules

If making your own bag, sew together two squares of muslin, leaving one side open.

Mix together the coconut oil and milk powder, then add the dried herbs or petals and essential oils. Spoon into the muslin bags and sew along the open edges, leaving a long thread to hang the bag on the bath tap under running water if you wish.

When you are ready for your bath, either hang the bag on the tap so the water runs through it, or place inside the bath as it fills. Step into the bath and relax! For a more intense effect, allow the bath bag to sit in the bath and continue to infuse. Discard the bag after use.

INDULGENT BATH TIMES

SOOTHING OATMEAL SOAK

This soothing bath soak is perfect for sensitive, itchy and fragile skin. The base of oats is soothing and moisturizing, and will help to reduce itching and soreness, while the essential oils are nourishing and calming for your nerves, helping to promote rest and relaxation.

2 x 15-cm squares of natural muslin (or a ready-made spice bag)
cotton thread
needle
1 tablespoon milk powder
2 tablespoons rolled oats
3 vitamin E capsules

If making your own bag, sew together the two squares of muslin, leaving one side open.

In a glass bowl, mix the milk powder and the rolled oats. Break open and add the vitamin E capsules. Combine thoroughly, then spoon into the muslin bag and sew along the top edge (or close by tying drawstrings on the ready-made bag).

Drop the bag into the running bath water, leave to infuse in the bath and relax.

CALMING LAVENDER BATH SOAK

Relaxing in a deep, warm bath is a great way to unwind from a particularly stressful day and is also a great opportunity for a soothing body treatment. This bath soak will soften and moisturize even the most sensitive skin – and if you relax in the bath just before bedtime, the lavender oil will help encourage a deep, restful sleep. For this treatment avoid introducing soaps into the bath water.

2 x 15-cm squares of natural muslin (or a ready-made spice bag)
1 tablespoon rolled oats
8 drops of lavender oil

If making your own bag, sew together the two squares of muslin, leaving one side open.

Spoon the rolled oats into the bag and add the lavender oil. Sew along the top edge or close by tying drawstrings on the ready-made bag.

When running a bath, tie the drawstring to the tap and allow the water to cascade over the bag to release the benefits of the oats and lavender oil. Alternatively, place the closed bag in the bath and allow it to float and diffuse as the bath fills – there is no need to remove the bag. Relax and soak for as long as time allows!

HANDMADE SOAP

The simplest method of making soap – referred to as 'melt and pour' – involves melting down a prepared soap base (see Buyer's Guide p. 112) and adding your own choice of fragrance and colour. All you need is the soap base, moulds and whatever you wish to add, such as dried flower petals or salt flakes. You can use food colouring and essential oils for fragrance. As a rough guide, use around 20 ml of fragrance per 1 k of soap base.

Depending on how many bars you want to make and the size of your moulds, cut off an appropriate amount of soap base and divide it into small chunks. Put these in a microwaveable bowl and place in the microwave. Do not overheat – the base just needs to melt, so heat it for a few seconds at a time to ensure it doesn't burn.

Once the soap base is fully melted, mix in your selected fragrance or colour, as well as any solid additions, such as dried flower petals, oatmeal or salt flakes.

Stir in your liquid additions quickly before a skin forms, then pour into your chosen moulds and allow to cool. You can place the moulds in the fridge to speed the process up.

Once cool, remove the soaps from the mould. Store at room temperature.

There are so many chemicals in commercial hair-care products that can strip your hair of its natural oils and upset the pH balance of your skin. Using everyday, natural ingredients will bring the shine and vitality back to your hair. From shampoo to colouring this chapter has everything you need for luscious locks.

Home-Made Shampoo	Beer Hair Treatment
Dry Shampoo	Chamomile Hair Rinse
Home-Made Conditioner	Lightening Treatment
Deep Conditioning Treatment	Darkening Treatment
Protein Hair Pack	Heat Protection
Glossing Treatment	Root-Lift Booster
Thickening Treatment	Beach Hair Salt
Mint Scalp Treatment	Water Spritz
Vinegar Hair Rinse	

HOLISTIC HAIR CARE

HOME-MADE SHAMPOO

Avoid stripping away natural oils and irritating the scalp with the gentle, nourishing formulation of this shampoo. Suitable for all hair types, this preparation has a gentle base with nurturing essential oils to form a blend that penetrates and nourishes each hair shaft for healthy, shiny results. Store in a glass jar away from direct sunlight.

100 ml liquid Castile soap
5 drops of lavender essential oil
3 drops of geranium essential oil
2 drops of lemon essential oil
1 vitamin E capsule
glass jar with lid

Add the liquid soap to a blender together with the lavender, geranium and lemon essential oils.

Break open the vitamin E capsule and add, then blend the mixture thoroughly. Pour into the glass jar.

Use about 1 tablespoon of shampoo to wash hair clean and fresh – a little more if your hair is longer or very thick. Always rinse clean in warm water and follow with Home-Made Conditioner (p. 66) for hair that shines with health and vitality.

DRY SHAMPOO

The popularity of dry shampoo has increased in recent years with the realization that it is the ideal beauty emergency treatment once the art of application has been mastered. An added benefit is that it can add volume and root lift to fine hair. This shampoo will leave hair looking and smelling clean and fresh. Store in a little glass bottle or clean spice jar.

4 tablespoons cornflour
1 tablespoon bicarbonate of soda
glass jar with lid

Combine the cornflour and bicarbonate of soda in the glass jar and shake vigorously to combine the ingredients.

To apply, pinch a small amount between fingers and sprinkle along the hairline. Massage through hair to allow the mixture to grab any excess oil, then brush through to remove the residue. For easy application, spoon the dry shampoo into a clean spice jar with a perforated top.

HOME-MADE CONDITIONER

This everyday, protein-rich conditioner produces gorgeous glossy locks and prevents tangles or damaged split ends. Make fresh each time from the prepared base. Store the base in a glass jar in the fridge.

for the base conditioner
2 tablespoons lecithin granules
50 ml spring water
50 ml sweet almond oil
1 tablespoon jojoba oil
1 teaspoon cocoa butter
glass jar with lid

for each conditioning treatment
1 teaspoon sweet almond oil
2 evening primrose oil capsules
2 drops of lavender essential oil
2 drops of geranium essential oil
small glass jar

Prepare the base for the conditioner by dissolving the lecithin granules in the spring water in a heatproof bowl over a pan of simmering water.

Add the sweet almond oil, the jojoba oil and the cocoa butter to the bowl and mix together thoroughly. Pour into a glass jar and store in the fridge.

To prepare fresh conditioner each time, melt together in a glass bowl over a pan of simmering water, 1 tablespoon of the base mixture together with an additional teaspoon of sweet almond oil.

Break open and add the evening primrose oil capsules along with the lavender and geranium oils, and mix well. Apply the conditioner to towel-dried hair after shampooing, comb through your hair and leave to absorb for 5 minutes. Rinse clean with warm water. Store any left-over conditioner in a glass jar.

DEEP CONDITIONING TREATMENT

For a super-rich nourishing remedy for dry, fragile or damaged hair try this blend to encourage new hair growth and bring a luscious gloss to dry, frizzy hair. Use the same base conditioner from Home-Made Conditioner (opposite) and customize it for a deep treatment.

1 tablespoon Home-Made Conditioner base
2 tablespoons sweet almond oil
4 drops of borage seed oil
2 evening primrose oil capsules
5 drops of calendula essential oil
3 drops of chamomile essential oil

In a glass bowl over a pan of simmering water, add the conditioner base and sweet almond oil.

Stir well before adding the remaining ingredients and pour into a glass storage jar. This should provide two or three treatments.

After shampooing, apply the conditioner to towel-dried hair, comb through carefully and leave for 10 minutes before rinsing in warm water.

PROTEIN HAIR PACK

12 g gelatine
220 ml spring water
1 teaspoon cider vinegar
3 drops of calendula essential oil
3 drops of sandalwood essential oil

Mix the gelatine and water well to create a smooth liquid, stir and leave to set to a gel-like consistency.

Add the vinegar and the calendula and sandalwood oils, and apply to the hair after shampooing. Leave to absorb for 10 minutes before rinsing.

GLOSSING TREATMENT

This glossing gel is the perfect de-frizz agent – in one step nourishing and helping to style locks to a sleek, shiny finish. This non-sticky gel is the ultimate natural hair styling product to create a glistening hair texture and a high-gloss, frizz-free result.

90 ml aloe vera gel
30 ml jojoba oil
12 drops of lavender essential oil
8 drops of sandalwood essential oil
medium dark-glass jar with lid

Mix all the ingredients thoroughly in the dark-glass jar to a smooth gel-like paste.

Apply the gel sparingly to your hair ends after washing and before blow-drying, and use a small quantity on the fingertips to pull through hair ends.

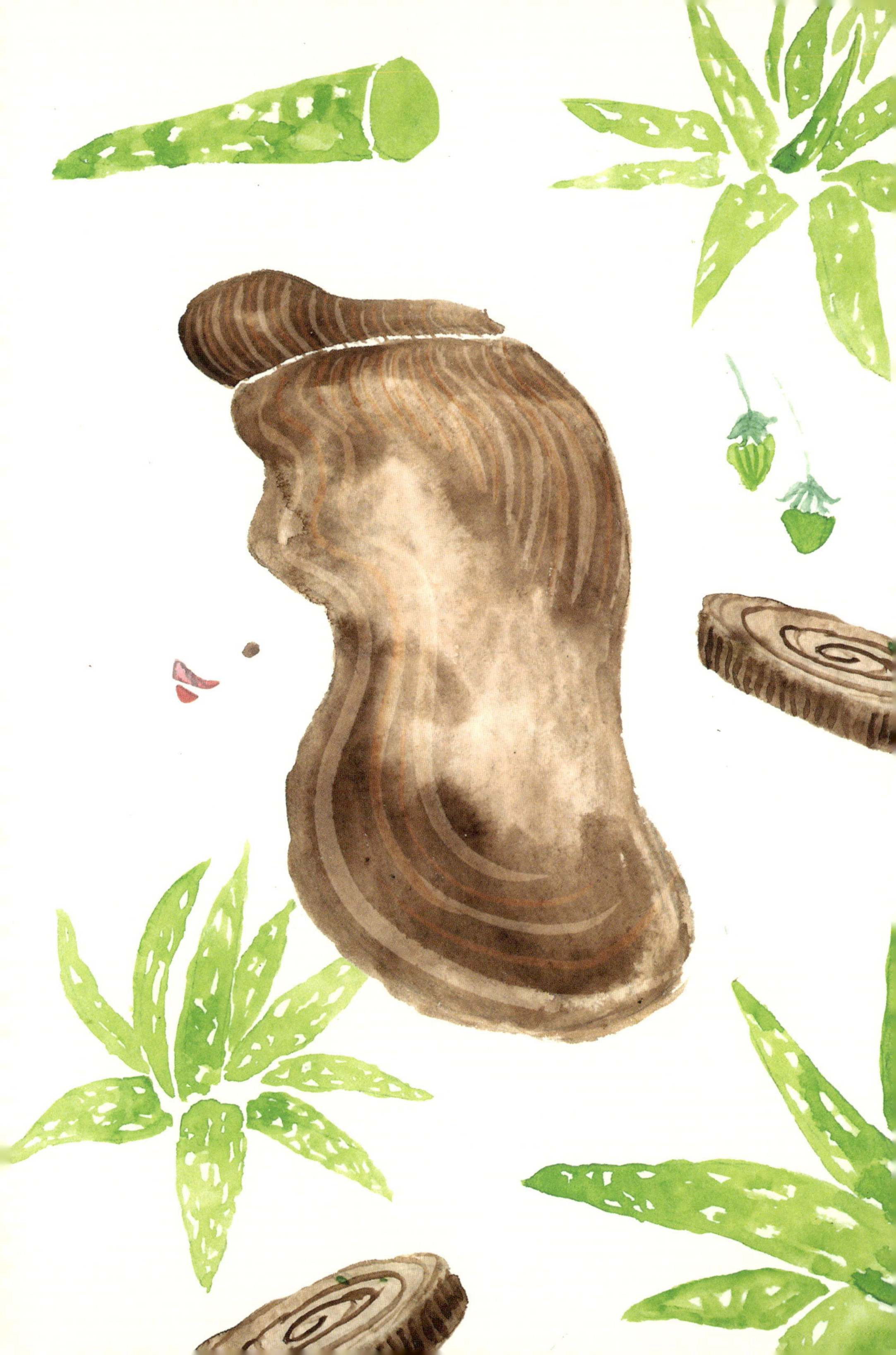

THICKENING TREATMENT

This protein-rich treatment mix boosts thinning hair and promotes lustrous hair growth and volume. Avocado is a superfruit, packed with vitamins A, B6, D and E plus magnesium, folic acid, amino acids, copper and iron – all boosting strong, thick hair growth and sleek conditioning. The egg white and wheatgerm oil provide protein-rich nourishment for the hair shaft to prevent hair fall and breakage. Rosemary essential oil stimulates blood circulation to the scalp and boosts hair follicle nutrition to encourage regrowth. Honey is a powerhouse of vitamins and acts as a humectant, attracting and retaining moisture in the hair shaft and minimizing dry, damaged frizz.

½ avocado
1 egg white
2 teaspoons honey
½ teaspoon wheatgerm oil
6 drops of rosemary essential oil

Mash the avocado (use whole fruit for long hair) and all the other ingredients to a smooth pulp.

Apply to your scalp and damp hair, and wrap with either plastic wrap and a warm towel or a shower cap. Leave to absorb for 30 minutes.

Shampoo the treatment out, then condition and style as normal. Repeat weekly for visible results.

MINT SCALP TREATMENT

This scalp-stimulating treatment can be used daily after conditioning. The mint and rosemary essential oils stimulate circulation to the scalp and encourage hair growth, while the lavender is gently healing.

5 drops of peppermint essential oil
3 drops of rosemary essential oil
5 drops of lavender essential oil
small dark-glass jar with lid
2 teaspoons vodka
2 tablespoons spring water

Mix the essential oils in the glass jar, swirl and add the vodka and water. Mix well and store out of direct sunlight. Apply regularly to the scalp using small, gentle rotations with your fingertips.

VINEGAR HAIR RINSE

Cider vinegar is a wonder ingredient for hair. Its acidity helps to seal the hair's cuticles, making it an ideal finishing rinse for stunningly shiny results. This rinse also helps restore the natural pH balance of a healthy scalp, while the essential oils penetrate deeply to produce glossy hair.

1 tablespoon cider vinegar
3 drops of lemon essential oil
25 ml spring water

Pour the cider vinegar into a small bowl, add the lemon essential oil, stir well and add the spring water.

After shampooing and conditioning your hair, rinse thoroughly, towel dry, then drench hair with the rinse. Finally, rinse with warm, fresh water. Dry and style as usual.

BEER HAIR TREATMENT

This hair rinse is ideal for dry and frizz-prone hair. The beer coats the hair with proteins to strengthen the shaft and protect against heat and sun damage. Rosemary boosts circulation to the scalp, while the lemon essential oil naturally cleanses and brightens for fresh and fragrant hair.

25 ml beer
5 drops of lemon essential oil
5 drops of rosemary essential oil

Mix the beer and lemon and rosemary essential oils in a small bowl.

Wash your hair with shampoo and conditioner, then rinse thoroughly. Massage the treatment through your hair, then rinse through with fresh water.

CHAMOMILE HAIR RINSE

This chamomile rinse is very easy to make and apply, and gently nourishes and enhances the light hues of fair hair, subtly highlighting without harsh chemicals. The effects are cumulative, so be sure to use this regularly for gradual effect.

6–8 chamomile teabags
freshly boiled water

Steep the tea bags in 1 litre of boiling water for 30 minutes to make a good, strong brew. Transfer the tea into a jug and add about 1 litre of cool water to make a diluted solution.

With your head over a large bowl in a basin or sink, slowly pour the diluted brew through the hair. Comb through to the ends, then pour the liquid back into the jug and repeat the rinsing and combing process three times. Make sure the solution soaks the scalp and hair roots.

With short hair, the solution can be spritzed into the hair with a pump dispenser bottle for ease. Allow the hair to absorb the final chamomile rinse by wrapping a towel around the head for 30 minutes before rinsing with warm water.

The gentle highlighting effect of the chamomile rinse can be further enhanced by exposure to the sun.

LIGHTENING TREATMENT

This timeless kitchen remedy has been used for centuries to create natural sun-kissed blonde highlights in fair hair. It is very easy to prepare, but experiment carefully with extended sun exposure or repeated applications to achieve lighter, brighter results. A general spritz will create overall sun-kissed highlights, while precision application can create a dramatic ombré effect.

500 ml very strong chamomile tea
125 ml very strong calendula tea
glass pump dispenser bottle
125 ml fresh lemon juice

Brew the chamomile and calendula teas for 30 minutes. Strain the liquid into the pump dispenser bottle together with the fresh lemon juice. Shake to mix thoroughly.

Spritz the solution on to clean, dry hair, applying the liquid only to the areas to be highlighted. Be sure to thoroughly saturate for best results. A natural balayage or sun-kissed look can be achieved by carefully coating the hair ends with the lemon mix.

The highlight effect is intensified by exposure to the sun. Allow it to absorb for 1 to 2 hours before washing hair thoroughly.

HOLISTIC HAIR CARE

DARKENING TREATMENT

Walnut powder is a natural colorant that can be bought online or in health-food stores. This easy rinse gently darkens hair colour with wonderful glossy results.

60 g black walnut powder
small muslin bag
freshly boiled water

Pour the walnut powder into the small muslin bag and steep in a bowl containing 1.5 litres of freshly boiled water. Leave for 6 hours or overnight.

Remove the muslin bag from the solution and discard. Pour the walnut rinse through the hair while showering and comb through. Allow your hair to dry naturally in sunlight, if possible, to create super dark coverage over colour-treated or grey hair.

This rinse can be repeated daily until the desired colour shade is reached, and repeated fortnightly to maintain coverage.

HEAT PROTECTION

Regular blow-drying or hair straightening with a heated appliance can cause hair to become dehydrated and lacking in natural shine. This formulation shields hair from the drying effects of any heated appliance, and treats hair with nourishing oils to restore shine and vitality. Store out of direct sunlight.

4 tablespoons macadamia nut oil
2 tablespoons grapeseed oil
small glass jar with lid

Pour the macadamia nut oil and grapeseed oil into the glass jar and shake to combine.

Wash and condition your hair as normal, then towel-dry before applying a little of the heat-protection solution to the ends of the hair. Work through to the ends with your fingers before styling.

ROOT-LIFT BOOSTER

Try this root-lift booster, which can also double as a styling gel, to add volume to fine or limp hair Store in the fridge.

¼ teaspoon gelatine powder
4 tablespoons just-boiled spring water
6 drops of essential oil, choose from:
  chamomile, for blonde or light hair
  lavender, to soothe the scalp
  rosemary, for darker hair
plastic bottle with nozzle

Place the gelatine powder into a glass bowl and add the spring water, stirring to dissolve. Leave to cool.

Refrigerate until partially set, then add your chosen essential oil and stir.

Pour into a plastic bottle with a nozzle for easy application and apply to your hair roots on wet or dry hair and massage gently before styling.

BEACH HAIR SALT WATER SPRITZ

Seawater can be very drying, but this treatment will guarantee silky, healthy hair and still supply beautiful sun-kissed beach hair. Extra simple to make, it avoids nasty chemicals and replaces sea salt, which can be drying, with Epsom salts to provide volume and texture in a blend that can be adapted to different hair types. Store in a dark-glass pump spray bottle out of direct sunlight.

dark-glass pump spray bottle
235 ml hot (not boiling) spring water
2 tablespoons Epsom salts (add more for a thicker/stiffer texture)
½ teaspoon sea salt
1 teaspoon aloe vera gel
½ teaspoon conditioner (p. 64) (for dry/coloured/damaged hair only)
10 drops lavender essential oil

Fill the glass pump spray bottle with the hot water, Epsom salts, sea salt, aloe vera gel, conditioner and lavender oil.

Replace the cap and shake vigorously for 2 minutes, or until the salts are dissolved.

After shampooing and conditioning, towel-dry the hair and spritz the solution to the full length of damp hair, scrunching dry to create loose, textured waves. For added volume, just spritz the hair when dry, concentrating on the roots, and leave overnight.

Spritz again in the morning and scrunch your hair for an all-day-long beach look.

HOLISTIC HAIR CARE

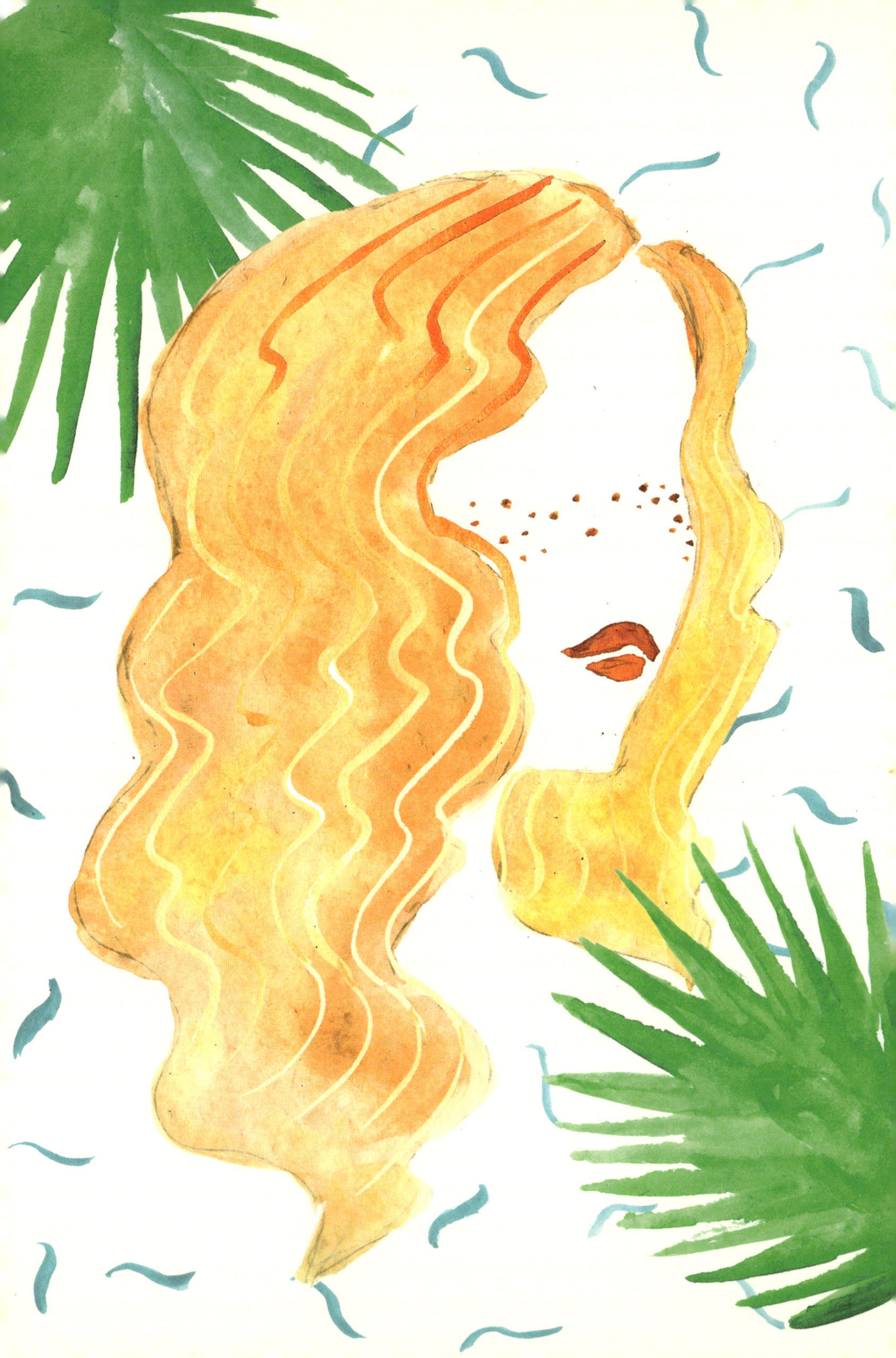

Complete your new, natural beauty regime with these luxurious finishing touches. Treat yourself to a home manicure and pedicure, or luxuriate in home-made body butter and oils. From head to toe this chapter has every aspect of your new beauty regime covered.

Lash Conditioner	Home Pedicure
Eyebrow Thickener	Foot Exfoliator
Teeth Whitener	Softening Foot Balm
Lip Buffer	Home Manicure
Natural Lip Plump	Nail Whitener
Natural Powder Blush	Cuticle Cream
Natural Lip Tint	Hand and Nail Cream
Body Butter	Nail Oil
Body Oil	

FINISHING TOUCHES

LASH CONDITIONER

Wearing mascara every day can leave eyelashes dry, brittle and highly susceptible to breakage. Try giving your eyelashes a weekend break from mascara and replace it with this indulgent treatment to strengthen, restore and encourage healthy growth. Use this conditioner morning and evening and in just one weekend lashes will look more luscious. Store in a small pot in the fridge.

2 tablespoons jojoba oil
2 tablespoons aloe vera gel
small pot or jar with lid
cotton buds

In a small glass bowl mix the jojoba oil and aloe vera gel and pour into the pot. Apply with a cotton bud along the base of the lashes, sweeping the length of the lashes, morning and evening, using a fresh cotton bud each time. Store in the fridge.

EYEBROW THICKENER

The eyebrows create a perfect frame for the face and the following recipe will help keep them full and healthy. Store in a small pot.

1 teaspoon cornflour
½ teaspoon cacao powder (unsweetened)
small pot with lid
cotton buds

Combine the cornflour and cacao powder and use a cotton bud to gently brush over the brows and blend. If eyebrows are dark, add more cacao powder to intensify the colour.

For an extra treatment at night time, swipe a little almond oil over brows to encourage healthy growth.

TEETH WHITENER

Mashed strawberries are renowned for their ability to naturally whiten teeth, but this teeth whitener recipe is even better. The bicarbonate of soda acts as a mild abrasive to rid teeth of stains, and its alkaline properties help neutralize acids and bacteria. The coconut oil helps reduce bacteria and promote healthy gums, while turmeric has anti-inflammatory properties. Store in glass jar in the fridge.

3 tablespoons ground turmeric
2 teaspoons bicarbonate of soda
2 tablespoons coconut oil
glass jar with lid

Combine the turmeric with the bicarbonate of soda. Add the coconut oil, then mix thoroughly and spoon into a glass jar.

Use a pea-sized amount on a clean toothbrush and brush your teeth in a soft, circular motion for 3 minutes, then rinse and spit several times. Although the turmeric is yellow your teeth will be shining white!

LIP BUFFER

Cracked and flaky lips are a common feature in cold wintry months or after a day at the beach in the summer sun. Lips have no oil glands and have very thin skin, so they need extra care to keep them soft, supple and kissable! This balm will keep your lips smooth and hydrated. Store in a small pot in the fridge.

1 teaspoon jojoba oil
1 teaspoon coconut oil
1 tablespoon honey
1 tablespoon brown sugar

Mix together the jojoba oil with the coconut oil, honey and sugar.

Spoon into a small pot. Apply the buffer using a fingertip, rubbing gently across the lips. Leave for 2 minutes for the oils to be absorbed, then rinse with warm water.

NATURAL LIP PLUMP

3 tablespoons coconut oil
2 tablespoons beeswax pellets
2 vitamin E capsules
½ teaspoon honey
12 drops of cinnamon essential oil

Mix the coconut oil and beeswax pellets in a glass bowl over a pan of simmering water until melted. Remove from heat, break open and add the vitamin E capsules to the bowl together with the honey and cinnamon oil. Mix thoroughly and pour into a small pot to harden. Apply as a regular lip balm. Store in a small pot in the fridge.

NATURAL POWDER BLUSH

All complexions benefit from a healthy, walk-in-the-country glow and one of the best ways to achieve this is to add a delicate flush of colour to the cheeks. This natural powder blush offers easily buildable colour so you can choose just a light blush or apply more to create a stronger look for evenings.

2 tablespoons arrowroot flour
1 teaspoon red-berry powder
raw cacao powder (optional)
small pot with a lid

Sieve the arrowroot flour into a small glass bowl and then slowly add the red-berry powder and mix.

Test the colour with a tiny pinch of the powder mix on the back of the hand until the desired shade is achieved. If the colour becomes too pink, add a little of the cacao powder to deepen the final shade. Once mixed, spoon into a small pot and it's ready to use.

Swirl a little of the powder on the apples of your cheeks with a blusher brush and slowly add more to build your perfect, healthy glow.

You may also choose to create two versions of this blusher: a lighter shade for daytime or summer and a deeper colour for evenings or winter.

NATURAL LIP TINT

A natural colour for lips and cheeks, this lip tint will add a hint of pretty pink in a nourishing formulation that will help keep lips hydrated throughout the day. Experiment with the ingredients to achieve your perfect natural shade. Store in a small pot in the fridge.

½ fresh raw beetroot
1 tablespoon coconut oil
1 vitamin E capsule
small pots with lids

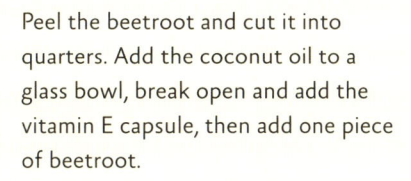

Peel the beetroot and cut it into quarters. Add the coconut oil to a glass bowl, break open and add the vitamin E capsule, then add one piece of beetroot.

Place the glass bowl over a pan of simmering water to heat the ingredients and encourage the beetroot juice to flow. Remove the beetroot piece when you are happy with the colour – or add more pieces to create a darker shade.

Allow the mixture to cool, then pour into small pots. Refrigerate in between uses: the tint will solidify in the fridge but will melt on the lips to leave a pretty, natural hint of colour.

BODY BUTTER

If skin is dry, a nourishing, luxurious moisturizing butter will bring instant comfort with its long-lasting, skin-nourishing benefits. Store in a glass jar out of direct sunlight.

4 tablespoons shea butter
2 tablespoons coconut oil
2 tablespoons almond oil
8 drops of essential oils, choose from:
  sweet orange
  rose
  ylang ylang
  lavender
glass jar with lid

To make the body butter base, melt the shea butter with the coconut oil and almond oil in a glass bowl over a pan of simmering water.

Remove from heat and add your chosen essential oil. Allow to cool in the fridge and as it starts to turn solid, blend with a hand blender until light and fluffy. Spoon into the glass jar.

BODY OIL

This nourishing body oil will boost the health of your skin with its clarifying and hydrating essential oils. Applying with circular massage strokes will stimulate your lymphatic drainage and boost circulation.

2 vitamin E capsules
30 ml sweet almond oil
5 drops of grapefruit essential oil
4 drops of cypress essential oil
3 drops of lavender essential oil
dark-glass bottle

Break open the vitamin E capsules into a glass bowl and add the sweet almond oil, grapefruit, cypress and lavender oils. Mix thoroughly and pour into a dark-glass bottle.

HOME PEDICURE

Feet are often the last to receive care and attention even though they are most likely to suffer more than any other part of the body from everyday stresses and strains! A weekly home pedicure will help to keep your feet and nails healthy and looking their very best even when they are hidden in socks and boots throughout winter. The benefits of a weekly foot massage all year round will also relax body and mind to promote general good health and a feeling of well-being.

handful of Epsom salts
10 drops of lavender essential oil

Fill a large bowl with warm water and add the Epsom salts and lavender essential oil. Lower your feet into the bowl and relax for about 10 minutes to allow the nails, cuticles and hardened skin to soften.

Massage each foot with Foot Exfoliator (p. 90), taking care to rub gently around the nails and cuticles. Use a pumice stone to gently remove any dry, hard skin around the heels.

Check your toenails and trim away any length, cutting straight across to avoid ingrowing nails. Gently push down and neaten cuticles with an orange stick.

Gently pat each foot dry, then massage with Softening Foot Balm (p. 91), taking care to separate and massage between the toes and knead underfoot to relieve any stresses. After a few pedicure treatments, cracked heels will disappear. Take your time and allow 5 minutes for each foot to stimulate circulation.

Finish with a fresh coat of nail polish, or polish nails lightly with a nail buffer for a more natural look.

FOOT EXFOLIATOR

Packed with over 70,000 nerve endings, feet respond very well to little treats such as this foot exfoliator. The calendula oil works to soften any hard skin or corns, while the lavender oil soothes swollen, tired feet and acts as a sweet-smelling antibacterial and healing agent. Make fresh each time for this weekly treatment.

1 teaspoon sweet almond oil
1 teaspoon medium ground sea salt
5 drops of calendula essential oil
3 drops of lavender or lemon essential oil

In a small bowl, mix the sweet almond oil and sea salt together with the calendula essential oil and lavender or lemon essential oil.

Soak your feet in warm water for 5 minutes, then apply the scrub mix to each foot in turn. Gently rub the mix all over each foot, paying attention to the heels, toes and balls, and concentrating carefully around each cuticle and nail.

Rinse your feet in the soaking bowl and allow to air-dry. Massage in a teaspoon of Softening Foot Balm (opposite) all over your feet and ankles. The lavender oil can be replaced with lemon essential oil for natural nail-brightening results.

SOFTENING FOOT BALM

A good foot massage is an essential part of a home pedicure regime – but is great at any time to reinvigorate mind, body and soul! This treatment is deeply moisturizing – therefore especially effective on cracked heels – and astringent with antibacterial properties that will make feet feel fresh and restored. For a more relaxing balm, replace the rosemary or spearmint oil with the same quantity of soothing chamomile or calming lavender oil. Store in a glass jar out of direct sunlight.

4 tablespoons coconut oil
3 tablespoons shea butter
8 drops of essential oil, choose from:
  rosemary
  spearmint
  chamomile
  lavender
glass jar with lid

Melt the coconut oil with the shea butter in a glass bowl over a pan of simmering water. Remove from the heat and add your chosen essential oil.

Pour into a glass jar. Scoop up a generous amount and smother each foot for a nourishing treatment. For very cracked heels, apply the balm and then wear thin, white cotton socks overnight.

HOME MANICURE

Good grooming always includes a perfect manicure with soft, smooth hands and expertly shaped nails. Recreating a salon-style result at home is achievable if you follow these five easy steps, which can become part of a weekly regime to condition hands and ensure healthy-looking nails.

handful of Epsom salts
10 drops of lemon essential oil

First remove any nail polish residue with an acetone-free remover, then neaten nails by filing into shape.

In a small bowl of warm water, mix the Epsom salts and lemon essential oil and soak each hand for 10 minutes to whiten and brighten your nails.

Gently push back the cuticles using an orange stick, then cleanse hands with Exfoliating Vibrancy Facial Scrub (p. 16) to remove any flaky dry skin. Then rinse in the warm hand soak.

Gently pat hands dry, then apply a coin-sized amount of Hand and Nail Cream (p. 95) and massage all over your hands and around the nails until completely absorbed.

To finish, apply a fresh coat of polish or use a nail buffer to lightly polish nails and stimulate circulation for a more natural style.

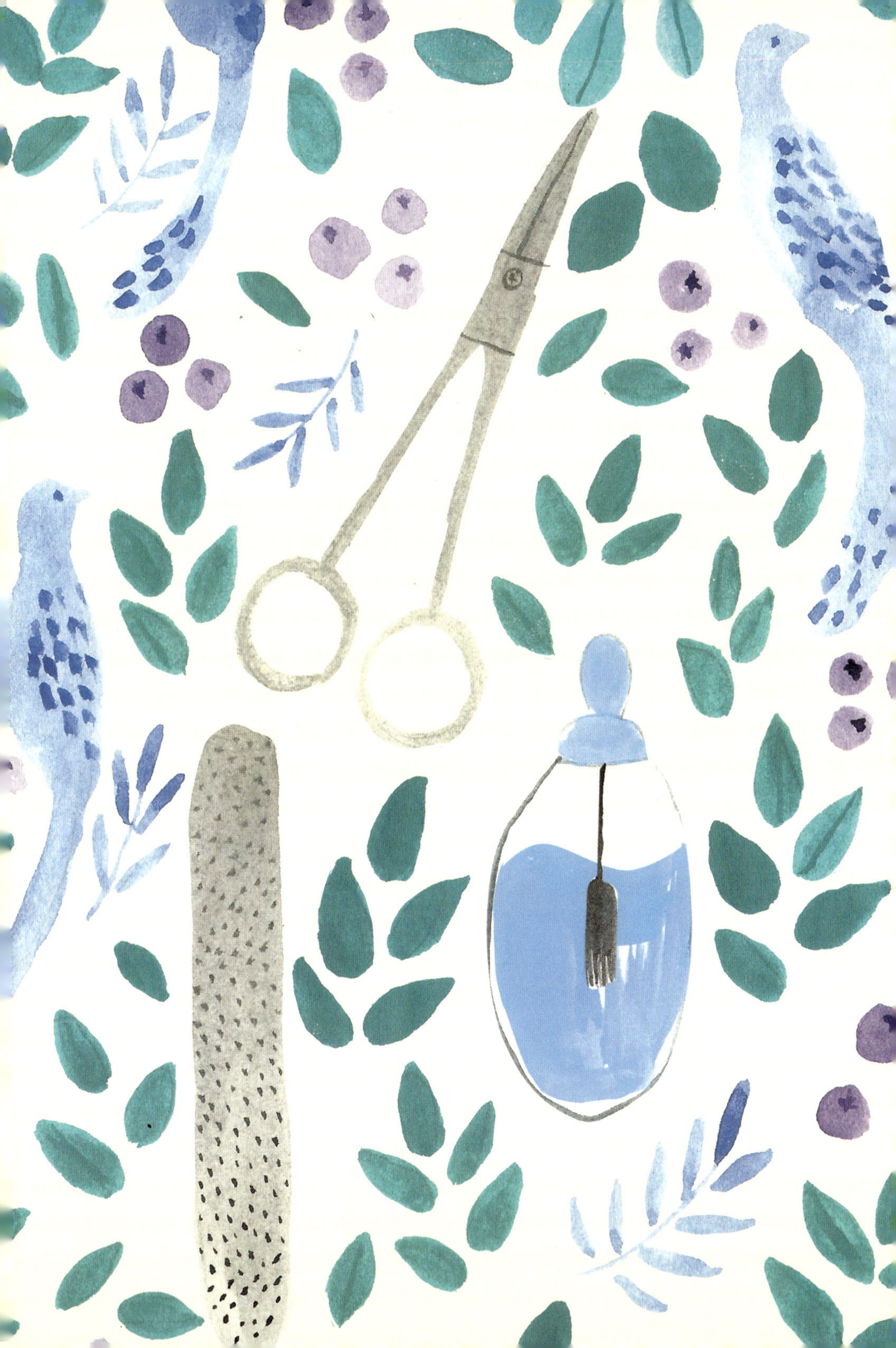

NAIL WHITENER

Regular nail polish wearers will understand the issue of yellowing nails. Restore a fresh, clean look with this whitening treatment that can be used weekly. Make fresh each time.

juice of ½ a lemon
2 teaspoons bicarbonate soda

Mix the lemon juice with the bicarbonate soda in a small bowl. Apply this paste to each fingernail and massage gently to remove stains.

Rinse with warm water, gently pat dry, then treat nails to a massage with Cuticle Cream (below).

CUTICLE CREAM

Ragged cuticles can ruin an otherwise perfectly groomed look – at worst they can catch and tear, leaving sore fingers that are open to possible infection. Cuticles should never be cut with scissors. Instead, massage gently with this cream and push back gently using an orange stick. Store in a small glass jar out of direct sunlight.

2 tablespoons shea butter
1 tablespoon coconut oil
1 teaspoon beeswax pellets
7 drops of lavender oil
small glass jar with lid

Melt the shea butter, coconut oil and beeswax pellets in a glass bowl over a pan of simmering water. Apply a thin layer of the cream to cuticles and fingertips at night before bed.

HAND AND NAIL CREAM

The hands are the first to show signs of ageing since they are exposed to all seasonal elements and are often neglected when it comes to applying sunscreen or protective skincare. An essential part of any beauty regime should include the application of a rich nourishing moisturizer to protect and nurture hands, and maintain strong, healthy nails. Massage a generous amount into the hands and nails at bedtime or use after washing dishes. Store in a glass jar in the fridge.

10 g cocoa butter
10 g beeswax pellets
30 ml sweet almond oil
2 evening primrose oil capsules
2 vitamin E capsules
5 drops of rose essential oil
2 drops of geranium essential oil
3 drops of lemon essential oil
glass jar with lid

Melt the cocoa butter with the beeswax pellets in a glass bowl over a pan of simmering water, then add sweet almond oil.

Break open the evening primrose oil capsules and vitamin E capsules, and pour into the mix, adding the rose, geranium and lemon essential oils. Mix well and pour into a glass jar.

The moisturizer can be made thicker by reducing the amount of sweet almond oil if preferred, or try adding a little more sweet almond oil if you prefer to use a pump dispenser.

NAIL OIL

For strong, healthy, blemish-free nails it is essential to nourish the entire nail, nail bed and cuticle. This nail oil will strengthen nails to prevent splitting, stimulate healthy growth and soften cuticles, making it easier to perfect the home manicure. Rosemary essential oil boosts circulation to promote growth, while the lemon essential oil will lighten and brighten the nail tips for a healthy look. Store in a glass jar away from direct sunlight.

10 ml jojoba or avocado oil
glass jar with lid
1 capsule evening primrose oil
8 drops of lemon essential oil
2 drops of rosemary essential oil

Pour the jojoba or avocado oil into a glass jar, break open and add the contents of the capsule of evening primrose oil and follow with the lemon and rosemary essential oils. Shake to mix thoroughly.

Massage into the fingernails and toenails at bedtime and leave overnight to achieve the best results. When applying nail polish, remember to thoroughly remove the oil to ensure even coverage.

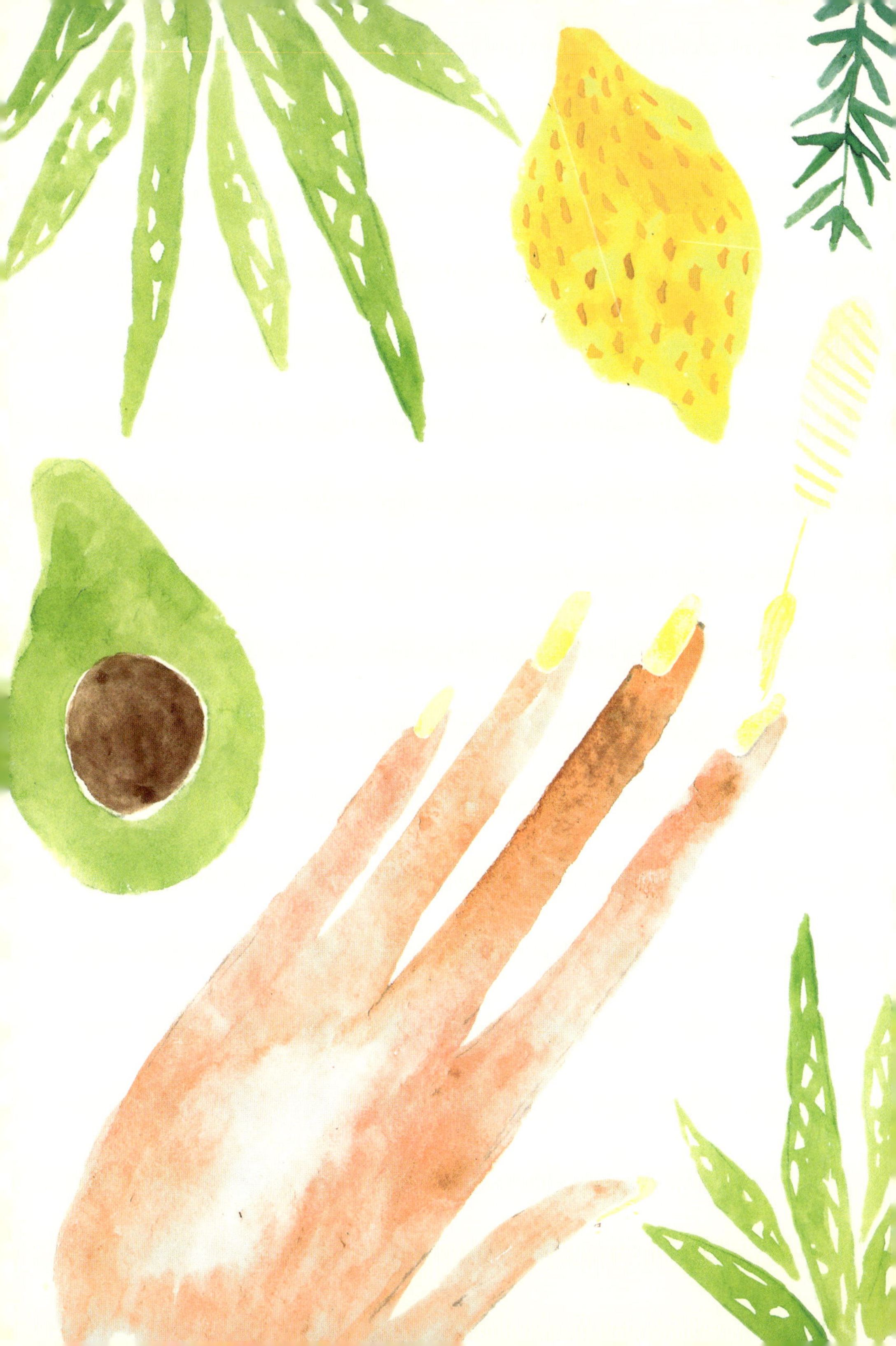

Our sense of smell is intimately linked with memory and emotion, and a stray scent of perfume can instantly transport us to a particular time or place. Create your own signature perfume or cologne that can evoke past memories or help create new ones. This chapter will also take you through using essential oils, which can be used for pleasure or as aromatherapy.

Home-Made Perfume	Home-Made Pillow Spritz
Home-Made Cologne	Aromatherapy Potpourri
Lavender Sachet	Blending a Massage Oil
Aromatherapy	Basic Massage Blends

SOOTHING SCENTS

HOME-MADE PERFUME

Customizing the perfect scent from individual essential oils is a highly personal and creative process to produce the ideal balance of top, middle and base notes. The top note creates the initial scent impression, the middle note is the heart and body of the perfume and the base note is the lingering aroma (often these base notes are effective fixatives to promote and hold a long-lasting fragrance). This solid perfume recipe is perfect for applying to pulse points – behind the ears, at the wrists, elbows and knees – for best but subtle effect. Easy to carry, this mix can be poured into any glass or metal container from small handbag size to larger dressing table proportions. It keeps well at room temperature but is best kept out of sunlight.

ESSENTIAL OILS

5 of each trio according to whether you are creating a feminine or masculine scent.

FEMININE MIX

top note: neroli, mid note: rose, base note: frankincense

MASCULINE MIX

top note: lemon, mid note: myrtle, base note: cedarwood

½ tablespoon shea butter
½ teaspoon cocoa butter
1 vitamin E capsule
1 tablespoon beeswax pellets
small glass bottle and glass or metal jars

In a small glass bottle, add 5 drops of each trio of essential oils, mix well and allow to mellow for a couple of days to allow the fragrance to develop and enhance in strength.

Melt the shea and cocoa butters, vitamin E and beeswax pellets in a glass bowl over a pan of simmering water. Mix thoroughly.

Add the essential oil blend to the bowl. Mix well and pour the mixture into glass or metal jars. Allow to cool and harden before use.

HOME-MADE COLOGNE

Making your own cologne is as simple as mixing three natural essential oils with alcohol and spring water, combined with experimentation, intuition, enthusiasm and sheer enjoyment. As with creating a solid perfume, you need to establish top, middle and base notes in your selection of essential oils. Proportions can be adjusted and alternative favourite scents added for a more complex olfactory experience.

SIMPLE FLORAL MIX
15 drops of sandalwood (base note)
20 drops of geranium (mid note)
15 drops of neroli (top note)

SIMPLE CITRUS MIX
10 drops of cedarwood (base note)
5 drops of vetiver (mid note)
30 drops of bergamot (top note)

70 ml vodka
30 ml spring water, or orange flower water if preferred
glass bottle or jar
paper coffee filter
glass pump spray bottle

Add the selected trio of essential oils and the vodka to the glass bottle or jar. Swirl gently to mix thoroughly. Leave for two days to develop out of sunlight.

Add the spring or orange flower water and mix gently until well diffused. Leave for four weeks, again out of sunlight. Pour through a paper coffee filter into the glass pump spray bottle.

Store out of direct sunlight and spritz on pulse points, taking care not to apply to delicate facial skin or sun-exposed body areas where the alcohol or citrus oils may cause skin irritation.

SOOTHING SCENTS

LAVENDER SACHETS

Fragrantly scented sachets are a wonderful way to keep your wardrobes and drawers smelling fresh. They also make a lovely home-made gift.

Cut a rectangle from a piece of pretty fabric, about the size of a postcard.

Sew a 1-cm hem along one long edge of the rectangle. This will be the top of your lavender bag, so make sure any pattern in the fabric is oriented the right way.

Fold the rectangle in half, with the right side of the fabric facing inward, making sure that the two short edges come together.

Starting from just beneath the hem, sew a 0.5-cm seam to join the two short edges of the fabric together. You should now have a fabric tube with the hemmed edge at the top.

Next, sew a 0.5-cm seam along the bottom edge of the tube to complete the bag. Turn the bag right-side out, pushing out the corners fully, and press with a hot iron.

Thread a length of narrow ribbon through the hem at the top of the bag to make a drawstring. You can tie the ribbon to a safety pin to guide it through.

Fill the bag with a spoonful or two of dried lavender and pull the drawstring to close it. Tie a double knot to keep it secure and make a bow to make it pretty. Replace the lavender about once a month.

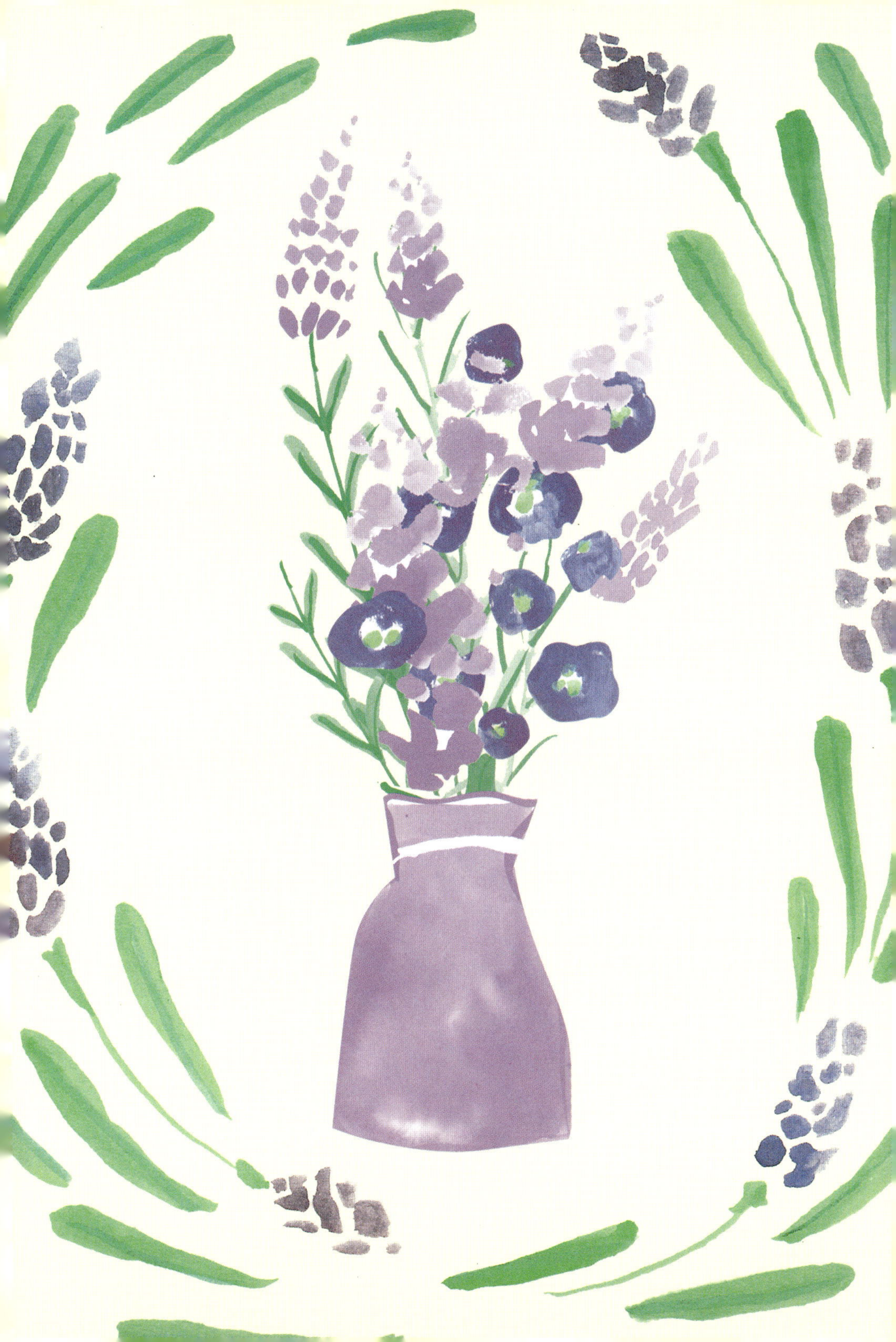

AROMATHERAPY

You may be surprised how much the power of fragrance can affect your general well being. Aromatherapy uses plant-based essential oils to shape moods and emotions.

Using Essential Oils

Essential oils are a wonderful way to bring the healing benefits of aromatherapy into your life. They can be added to a hot bath, used to make potpourri, burned in oil burners or used as a massage oil. Essential oils should always be diluted using a base carrier oil (vegetable oils such as olive, avocado, sweet almond or grapeseed) before applied directly to the skin.

Lavender
To help insomnia and to calm and soothe, add 4 to 8 drops to a warm bath, or put 2 drops on your pillow at bedtime.

May Chang
To help increase energy levels, lift your mood and raise low spirits, put 5 to 6 drops in an oil burner, or 2 drops together with 2 drops of frankincense oil in your bath for an energizing soak.

Rosemary
To stimulate and invigorate during busy work periods, mix 10 drops with a base carrier oil and rub on your hands and feet to help you think clearly.

AROMATHERAPY BATH BLENDS

Strictly speaking, an aromatherapy bath is not a cleansing process – ideally, it should follow a shower – it is a therapeutic treatment in itself to promote the absorption of specific essential oils for mood enhancement or therapeutic remedy. Try these different blends for effect.

SOOTHING SPIRITUAL
2 drops of geranium essential oil
2 drops of mandarin essential oil
2 drops of frankincense essential oil

PURIFYING DETOXIFICATION
2 drops of grapefruit essential oil
2 drops of peppermint essential oil
2 drops of juniper essential oil

MUSCLE AND JOINT EASE
2 drops of rosemary essential oil
2 drops of marjoram essential oil
2 drops of lavender essential oil

Fill the bath with hot water. Add 4 to 6 drops of essential oil direct from each bottle. For an added touch of relaxation, enjoy a candle-lit soak (be sure to light candles just before you step into the bath and never leave naked flames unattended).

Relax and soak for 15 to 20 minutes, breathing in the essences and allowing the oils to absorb through the skin. Avoid using soaps or cleansers in the bath. The non-dispersible essential oils will cling to the body in a fine layer. Carefully step out and gently pat dry and apply a light body oil or nourishing body butter.

Alternatively, the essential oils can be diluted in a tablespoon of full-fat milk and poured into the running bath to disperse the oils throughout the bath water and avoid any risk of splashing to the eyes or face.

SOOTHING SCENTS

HOME-MADE PILLOW SPRITZ

The benefits of regular, good-quality sleep are well documented for optimum health, beauty and well-being. Trying to sleep in times of stress and enjoying a night of unbroken rest can be a nightmare. Literally. This night-time pillow spritz features the soothing and calming properties of lavender and Roman chamomile essential oils to help promote rest and relaxation. Store in a small glass pump spray bottle away from direct sunlight.

small glass pump spray bottle
25 ml spring water
1 teaspoon high-proof vodka
15 drops of lavender essential oil
5 drops of Roman chamomile essential oil

In a small glass pump bottle, mix the vodka with the lavender and Roman chamomile oils. Add the spring water, replace the cap and shake thoroughly before each use.

To reduce stress and encourage sleep, spritz your pillows with this treatment before sliding into bed and sinking into a blissful, precious night's sleep.

You can also use this spritz as a refreshing general linen spray on sheets, towels and laundry.

AROMATHERAPY POTPOURRI

For appearance: dried flowers, leaves and cones
For fragrance: fruit slices, whole spices and a few drops of essential oils
large jar with lid

First, select your ingredients, then mix together in a large bowl until you're happy with both the look and scent. Enjoy experimenting with this.

Transfer the mix to the jar, screw on the lid and leave in a cool, dark place for several weeks to let the scents infuse and intensify. Stir every few days and check the aroma's progress – if the scent isn't strong enough, add a drop or more of your chosen oils and leave for longer.

When ready, arrange your potpourri in a decorative bowl or basket, then place it wherever you most want a subtle touch of aromatherapy in your home.

When the scent begins to fade, add another drop or two of essential oil and stir to refresh.

POSSIBLE COMBINATIONS

Warm and spicy: dried, chopped orris root, dried orange slices, whole cloves, whole star anise, cinnamon sticks, sweet orange or ylang ylang essential oil.

Light and zesty: dried, chopped orris root or dried lavender, dried lemon slices, dried rose petals, dried geranium leaves, lemon or lavender oil.

BLENDING A MASSAGE OIL

Choose a nourishing cold-pressed carrier oil that will enhance the skin and promote a sumptuous sense of relaxation and indulgence such as sweet almond, grapeseed or rosehip oil. Jojoba is the closest to natural sebum and produces an easily absorbed penetrative carrier oil with a soft musky aroma. Sweet almond oil is a soothing oil rich in vitamins and proteins for inflamed dry skins. Apricot kernel oil is excellent for sensitive ageing skin, rich in vitamins and minerals.

To make your own massage oil, first decide which scents soothe or invigorate you – do you prefer a light and floral smell, zesty and fruity, or more woody and spicy fragrances?

Once you have selected your carrier and essential oils, mix them together as per the ratio recommended on the essential oil bottle – this will vary from oil to oil. If storing your massage blend for future use, do so in a dark-glass bottle away from direct heat or sunlight.

BASIC MASSAGE BLENDS

If you aren't sure where to start with your own scented massage oils, these suggestions are old favourites for relaxation, energizing and cool-down.

Pour approximately 20 ml of the base oil for a full-body application into a glass jar. Add 20 drops of essential oils in total.

Mellow Relaxation Blend

8 drops of chamomile essential oil
6 drops of cedarwood essential oil
4 drops of mandarin essential oil
2 drops of patchouli essential oil

Post-exercise Muscle Blend

8 drops of lavender essential oil
6 drops of peppermint essential oil
6 drops of eucalyptus essential oil

Uplifting Energy Blend

10 drops of lemon essential oil
10 drops of rosemary essential oil
6 drops of lime essential oil
4 drops of lavender essential oil

Gently swirl the oils to combine and apply to the body in long, slow, soothing strokes, carefully 'insisting' on areas of dry skin such as ankles, knees and elbows, and areas of general tension.

Allow the oils to be absorbed before getting dressed. Store any unused blended oil out of direct sunlight for up to one week.

SOOTHING SCENTS

INDEX

after-sun gel 44
almond oil 14, 23, 88
almond and
  oatmeal scrub 32
aloe vera 10, 13, 33, 44, 68, 78, 82
aloe vera moisturizer 13
anti-cellulite
  body tonic 42
apple and
  thyme cleanser 10
aromatherapy
  bath oils 105
  potpourri 107
  using essential oils 104
avocado 18, 33, 34, 70, 96, 104

basic massage blends 109
bath bags 58
bath bombs 56
bath milk 48
bath oils 105
bath salts 54, 55
bath soak 60
beach hair salt
  water spritz 78
beeswax 14, 34, 35, 85, 94, 95, 100
beeswax moisturizer 14
beer hair treatment 72
blush, 86
body butter 88
body cream 38
body mask 40
body mist 39
body oil 88
body scrub 32, 33

body tonic 42
body wash 52
borage oil 11, 67
brightening facial peel 17
brightening fruit facial 22
bubble bath 50, 51

calming lavender
  bath soak 60
Castile soap 36, 50, 51, 52, 64
citrus body wash 52
chamomile 24, 55, 73, 74
chamomile bath salts 55
chamomile hair rinse 73
clay body mask 40
cleanser 10, 11
cocoa butter 34, 66, 95, 100
coconut and lavender body
  cream 38
coconut oil 13, 19, 23, 26, 30, 35, 36, 38, 58, 84, 85, 87, 88, 91, 94
cologne 101
conditioner 66, 67, 82
cooling and rejuvenating
  face and body mist 39
cuticle cream 94

darkening treatment 76
deep conditioning
  treatment 67
deodorant 45
detoxifying clay
  body mask 40
dry shampoo 65

energizing face pack 20

epsom salts 48, 54, 55, 78, 89, 92
essential oils 54–55
evening primrose oil
  capsules 27, 44, 66, 67, 95, 96
exfoliator 16, 90
exfoliating vibrancy
  facial scrub 16
eye bag blitz 23
eyebrow thickener 83

face and body mist 39
face pack 18, 20
facial 19, 22, 24
facial peel 17
facial steamer 24
foot balm 91

grapeseed and borage
  oil cleanser 11
gentle rose
  water toner 12
glossing treatment 68
glycerine 50
green clay powder 19, 20, 40
green tea face cleanser 10

hair pack 67
hair treatment 68–76
hand and nail cream 95
handmade soap 61
heat protection 77
home pedicure 89
home-made cologne 101
home-made
  conditioner 66
home-made moisturizer 3

home-made shampoo 64
home-made perfume 100
home-made
　pillow spritz 106
honey 17, 18, 22, 52,
　70, 85
intensive dry
　skin balm 35
jojoba oil 10, 19, 20, 36, 44,
　52, 66, 68, 82, 85, 96, 108
lash conditioner 82
lavender
　calming lavender
　　bath soak 60
　coconut and lavender
　　body cream 38
　lavender sachet 102
lemons 17, 74, 94, 104
lip buffer 85
lip plump 85
lip tint 87
loofah 31
lovely legs
　shaving balm 36

making a loofah 31
manicure 92
massage blends 109
massage oil 108
mint scalp treatment 71
moisturizer 13, 14, 34
mud pack 19

nail cream 95
nail oil 96
nail whitener 94
natural after-sun gel 44
natural eye mask 23
natural face packs 18
natural deodorant 45
natural lip plump 85

natural lip tint 87
natural powder blush 86
natural spot
　treatments 27

oats 32, 59, 60
oatmeal soak 59
olive oil 14

pedicure 89
perfume 100
pillow spritz 106
potpourri 107
powder blush 86
protein hair pack 67

root-lift booster 77
rose bath milk 48
rose water 12, 18, 19, 34

scalp treatment 71
sea salt skin buffer 30
shampoo 64, 65
shea butter 26, 36, 88, 91,
　94, 100
soap 61
softening foot balm 91
soothing oatmeal soak 59
spot treatments 27
strawberries 18, 22, 24
strawberry facial
　steamer 24
sugar body scrub 33
sweet almond
　bubble bath 51
sweet almond oil 35, 44, 51,
　66, 67, 83, 88, 90, 95, 108

teeth whitener 84
thickening treatment 70
toner 12
tonic 41, 42

using bath salts 54

vinegar hair rinse 71
vitamin E capsules 14, 32,
　35, 52, 58, 59, 64, 85, 87,
　88, 95, 100
vodka 41, 42, 45, 71,
　101, 106

witch hazel 51
whitener 84, 94

INDEX

111

Buyer's Guide

Many of the ingredients used in this book are readily available at supermarkets and health-food stores. Some of the more specialist ingredients such as green clay powder, liquid Castile soap and lecithin granules are available from health food stores such as Planet Organic and Holland & Barrett, as well as online retailers. Essential oils can be purchased from pharmacies and health and beauty stores. Online retailers also sell a range of essential oils.

Safety Notes and Precautions

Before handling any ingredients, be sure to wash your hands thoroughly and sterilize tools with boiling water to eliminate bacteria that could contaminate your products.

Always test the product on a small area of skin first and take care when applying any treatment to the sensitive eye area. These recipes include only natural ingredients and are less likely to irritate sensitive skin than some of the chemicals found in over-the-counter preparations, however, if you experience any itching or redness, rinse the affected area with clean water immediately. These fresh and natural recipes do not contain the chemical preservatives that are found in store-bought items therefore not all products suggested here will keep well for a period of time.

If the recipe includes a foodstuff, then it is best to make a single batch and use it all in one go. Other recipes might keep for a short while, but remember that all these fresh and natural treatments have a much shorter shelf life than commercial products.

It is best to store products that will keep in the fridge, as indicated with the recipe. Try to use opaque and airtight containers when storing products. Dispensing bottles with plastic spouts are perfect, but take care to clean and sterilize them with boiling water before filling. Always use a spatula or a spoon to transfer your products to sterilized containers. As an extra precaution it is wise to label products as you make them with the name, date of preparation and key ingredients.